SHYAM BENEGAL (1934–2024) was a visionary Indian filmmaker who pioneered the country's parallel cinema movement in the 1970s and 1980s. His debut feature, *Ankur* (1974), offered a searing critique of the caste system and rural feudalism, earning both national and international acclaim. Benegal's diverse filmography includes acclaimed works such as *Nishant* (1975), *Manthan* (1976) and *Bhumika* (1977), which explored social issues with depth and sensitivity. Throughout his career, he was known for his exceptional storytelling, realistic portrayal of characters, and profound cinematic depth. Benegal's contributions to cinema were recognized with numerous accolades, including the Dadasaheb Phalke Award, India's highest honour in film. His legacy continues to inspire filmmakers and audiences alike.

SATYAJIT RAY (1921–1992) was a writer, illustrator, and one of the greatest filmmakers of the twentieth century who brought world recognition to Indian cinema. Noted for his humanism, versatility, and detailed control over his films and their music, Ray received several awards from film festivals at Cannes, Berlin, Venice and Moscow, as well as an honorary Oscar for lifetime achievement in 1992.

THE INDIA LIST

Satyajit Ray

A FILM BY
SHYAM BENEGAL

Script reconstructed by
ALAKNANDA DATTA
and
SAMIK BANDYOPADHYAY

LONDON NEW YORK CALCUTTA

Seagull Books, 2025

© Seagull Books, 1988

See 'A Note on the Illustrations' below for copyright information
on the images used in this volume.

First published in English translation by Seagull Books, 1988

ISBN 978 1 80309 540 0

British Library Cataloguing-in-Publication Data
A catalogue record for this book is available from the British Library

Typeset by Seagull Books, Calcutta, India
Printed and bound by Hyam Enterprises, Calcutta, India

CONTENTS

Introduction   *vii*
A Note on the Illustrations   *xii*

Satyajit Ray: A Film by Shyam Benegal   1

Conversations   149

Introduction

Ray, we have been told, would have liked this film to be more Benegal than Ray, more of an evaluation of or response to his entire corpus. I recall Benegal thinking aloud on the same lines after a spell of shooting. I have never asked him why he changed the thrust. Was it the sheer clarity of Ray's articulation that took over at a certain point and shaped the film the way it now is? For in what is perhaps his most comprehensive interview till date, Ray, speaking to Benegal, lays bare with remarkable candour all the elements that have gone into the making of that formidable body of work that represents as it stands an enlightened liberal's perception of the history of modern India, retold in terms of education as a value in itself triumphing over the vestiges of caste-bound orthodoxy, only to go under eventually as ruthless commercialism asserts itself out of the same bourgeois value system.

Benegal recognizes the departure that *Sadgati* is, with its almost naturalistic energy directed to an exposure of the exploitations of caste: 'I mean the film comes through with a tremendous amount of power and strength, and you do see oppression of a particular kind in full force. It isn't the kind of your gentle, the more ironic look at things.' But Ray would not acknowledge it as so much of a departure: 'It's just that the story called for that kind of treatment because that force, that anger is already there in the original story. And it seemed absolutely right for this particular story . . . I really don't know, I haven't worked it out whether this is a sort of inner change in myself, a looking at things in a more harsh sort of way than in an oblique way.' When I interviewed Ray for the National TV for the TV premiere of *Sadgati*, I found him more committed to a resolve to make at least a few more films directly on the rural/tribal realities. The *Sadgati* experience had been a kind of discovery not for Ray's audience alone, but for Ray himself too. And one of the stories he was considering seriously immediately after *Sadgati* was Mahasweta Devi's *Bichhan*.

In fact, though Ray tells Benegal: 'it's exactly how Premchand conceived the story, I've made almost no change [to the story] except perhaps add a few scenes here and there', there had been an overlay of irony in the story amounting almost to a cruelly mocking denunciation of the submission and endurance and acquiescence of the outcastes. Ray, in his film, had dispensed with the mockery which was there in the narratorial voice that frames the Premchand story. Ray's tonal shift gives the narrative a charge that is more direct than the bitter irony of the original.

In 1970, with *Pratidwandi*, Ray moved away finally from the area that he had defined for himself in the Apu trilogy and the films that followed immediately—the experience of a culture, primarily rural and still maybe loosely rooted in feudalism, evolving into the urban under the impact of colonial education. In a 1980 interview, even as I was telling Ray: 'in the earlier films like the Apu Trilogy or *Devi*, though ostensibly set in the village, there is a looking forward to the city, a search for the roots that the city has in the villages, the village that lies underneath the urban mind of Calcutta, which has yet to assume what we would identify more definitely as an entirely urban sensibility . . .', Ray interrupted me to add, '*Aranyer Dinratri* too is really about the city.' But with *Pratidwandi*, Ray seemed to have *reached* the city at last. The forward-looking values that Ray had been celebrating in his first phase of filmmaking—the reaching out to a rational conscience—seemed to have collapsed in a terrible morass of buying and selling in the nightmare world of his Calcutta Tetralogy.

In what Samar Sen, poet and radical journalist, described as Ray's descent 'to the lower depths, not of poverty, but degradation', the ideals that had inspired the dreamy-eyed Apu appeared grotesquely unreal. Benegal asks Ray: 'Would you say that you knew that the environment was changing around you, and there was the effect of that on you?' Ray replies, 'That did happen towards the end of the sixties, the early seventies. I could describe that as a period in which you strongly felt certain changes taking place, almost in the day to day existence you felt it, and you felt without that you couldn't make a film.' 1970, the *Pratidwandi* year, was a kind of watershed. Six years later, Samar Sen would be asking: 'How does one explain the change in Satyajit?' Then another six years, another interview, and I was already asking him: 'Films that really represent your expression have gone probing into problems, into larger situations, very often historically determined situations, into basic human relationships. But haven't you been doing only lightweight films for a fairly long time now from before *Shatranj* and since? . . . In your sequence of the films made in the seventies, you explored some of the most significant problems associated with middle class existence in Calcutta.

Do you think you have exhausted the whole range of these problems? Would you say you do not see at the moment any problem of the same significance demanding cinematic projection?' Ray answered quite firmly: 'I do not see any at the moment. I can't find any.' But then a couple of minutes later he would be telling me, 'I don't feel inspired right now.'

In a moving defence of his work in the late seventies, Ray told me in the course of this interview:

> Now let's see what I've made since *Shatranj*—*Jai Baba Felunath*, and my latest, *Heerak Rajar Deshey*. You must have noticed this trend with me of spending all my time outside cinema for children, writing for them, illustrating

for them. This has now gone on for nearly twenty years. Our *Sandesh* is now twenty years old . . . My work for children, which surfaced in the cinema for the first time in *Goopy Gyne Bagha Byne,* I enjoy immensely. In fact I have been feeling this other need more and more over the years beyond the urgency of what you call probing into problems—always at the back of my mind—to reach a larger audience. After making films for twenty years—twenty-five years—we haven't been able to reach an audience substantially large. When we see cheap films at a very average level of craftsmanship finding large audiences, we cannot just ignore the phenomenon. We came into films twenty or twenty-five years ago. But what have we achieved through our work over all these years? There has been the development of a certain kind of appreciation at the Film Society level. But that remains too limited to be really significant. What we call the audience remains far beyond it . . . They lie there somehow as an amorphous mass, far and absolutely beyond our circle. What do they want from cinema? We often ask ourselves: can't we do something for them, not necessarily going for all those cheap things or making compromises? This has been a perennial problem. Making films for children that could work at several levels, as in *Goopy Gyne,* and as definitely in *Heerak Rajar Deshey,* could be an answer. That way I could entertain the children, give the more intelligent and sophisticated adult spectators something to respond to with appeals at several levels. It's worthwhile to carry on with experiments in that direction . . . But that does not mean that I have moved away altogether to that end. Two films—they are nothing absolute. If you take a maker's complete oeuvre, two films are really nothing. There can be a radical change of direction after these. Larger perspectives can open up immediately. When you look

back at these ten years hence, you will find these repre-
senting just a passing phase, one of those phases.

(*Cinewave,* 1 January 1981)

The 'change of direction' came in 1981 itself, with *Pikoo* and *Sadgati*.
Benegal opens his film with Ray shooting *The Home and the World*,
and goes back to the beginnings of a man born in an almost arche-
typal 'renaissance' family, growing in a rich ambience drawing on
Western classical music, Santiniketan, drawing and painting, the
first film society in Calcutta, Renoir and Pudovkin and Cherkasov,
the world of children and their tastes, and a political setting that
turned more and more complex—to make a rich oeuvre of films in
which he claims: 'One thing which I have tried to do is not to repeat
myself thematically.' In his long interview, Ray opens up in a manner
in which he has not opened up ever before, and that would perhaps
be the greatest compliment for Benegal, who has treated Ray more
as an elder colleague and fellow worker than as a master.

SAMIK BANDYOPADHYAY

A Note on the Illustrations

As the reader will see, we have gone beyond Benegal's film to make the section of plates an archival selection of not so accessible material mostly created by Ray, and some related to him and his work. The one person who has contributed most to this section is Nemai Ghosh, regular and exclusive stills photographer of Ray's films for more than a decade now, with his excellent personal archive of Ray visuals. While the photo credits for all the stills from Benegal's film and from Ray's own *Ghare Bairey*, *Sadgati*, *Pikoo*, *Goopy Gyne Bagha Byne*, *Pratidwandi*, *Aranyer Dinratri*, *Shatranj ke Khiladi* and *The Inner Eye* are Ghosh's, most of the Ray sketches, designs and illustrations are reproduced here by his courtesy. The portraits and caricatures of Picasso, Dilipkumar and Nargis, the portraits of Ray as a child, and with Bergman, also come from his collection.

The stills from the Apu Trilogy, *Jalsaghar* and *Devi*, and the sketches from *Apur Sansar* are reproduced by courtesy of Satyajit Ray himself. The shot of Ray, Antonioni and Kurosawa in front of the Taj Mahal was taken by Sandip Ray.

The photographs of Pudovkin and Cherkasov at the Calcutta Film Society in 1952, and of Ray shooting *Aranyer Dinratri* are from the collection of the Society, who have kindly permitted us to reproduce them.

Shyam Benegal gave us a copy of a credits card set in Ray Roman, and a bromide of a page from Ray's *Pather Panchali* scenario.

Ray's sketches and covers for Signet Press publications like *Aamantir Bhenpu*, *Duranta Dupur*, *Naam Rekhechhi Komal Gandhar*, *Jonakira* and *Aapan Katha*, and the sketches by Sukumar Ray are reproduced by courtesy of Nilaksha Gupta and the Signet Press.

Ray's sketch of Eisenstein was made by him for the Eisenstein Cine Club, Calcutta, by whose kind permission it is reproduced here.

The early photograph of Ray briefing Karuna Banerjee on the sets of *Pather Panchali* was shot by Bansi Chandragupta, art director on all Ray's early films and *Shatranj*.

The first credits come on, with Ray's off-screen instructions to the crew on the sets of *Ghare Bairey* (*The Home and the World*), till he appears on screen, making a V sign to the crew not visible at first, a curio in his other hand, the camera following him on a trolley from right to left, to right, and to left again, bringing the piano in view at right of frame, with a member of the crew tuning it, and the rest of the crew, bustling around. Ray turns away from the camera after making the sign, but comes round almost at once to face it. A member of the crew holds a curio up to him, but he rejects it: 'No, it won't do there.'

CREDITS: FILMS DIVISION PRESENTS

  SATYAJIT RAY

  BY SHYAM BENEGAL

> RAY (*off*): Turn it a little to this side . . . Place it with its back to the wall . . . we'll need two of them . . . a little more to the side . . . go a little further . . . still further . . . go on . . . I'll tell you when to stop . . .

Cut to credits again, with ASSISTANTS.

> SOUMENDU ROY (*off*): Keep the lights low . . .

Ray moves in from right to left, a curio in hand, towards a table with a marble top, in medium shot, almost entirely back to camera, till he places the object on the table, which now displays an antique clock, flanked by two porcelain vases, under a picture in an ornamental frame on the wall above. As the camera moves, one catches glimpses of curtains that underline the period setting, till at the close of the shot Ray faces the camera looking at the set, pointing towards it.

RAY: Remove the small one—now . . .

MEMBER OF THE CREW: Let's have one of these here, the other there . . .

RAY: Wait a minute, we won't need it today . . . Let's see what the background is . . .

Cut to credits again.

CREDITS: PRODUCTION EXECUTIVE: RAJ PIUS
             PRODUCTION CONTROLLER: DILIP BANERJEE

SOUMENDU ROY (*off*): Let's have the floor clear.

RAY (*off*): Fine.

Ray in the foreground at right, Soumendu Roy in the background.

SOUMENDU ROY: Will this be here?

RAY: No. It won't be in the shot. I'll remove it.

VOICE (*off*): Bhola, remove this, and bring the piano here.

Ray comes into close-up, picking his teeth, tense, Soumendu Roy behind him.

Credits again.

CREDITS: FIRST ASSISTANT DIRECTOR: DEV BENEGAL

RAY (*off*): It won't look right there.

Ray, in low medium shot, in profile, adjusts his spectacles before he raises his wrist closer to his eyes to look at the watch.

CREDITS again.

CREDITS: EDITING: BHANUDAS DIVKAR

Ray and Victor Banerjee in medium shot, facing each other, Soumendu Roy between them. Ray scrutinizes Victor's make-up, feels his head all over, patting the hair down, even bends on his knees to take a closer look at the latter's face from beneath the chin. He is obviously not quite satisfied, and asks Victor to remove his moustache, the camera moving from one to the other all along to register reactions.

> RAY: Wait a bit. Keep it covered. It's difficult to decide. I'd prefer it slightly browner. It's black. Somehow it doesn't belong to you.

> VICTOR: Shall I remove it?

> RAY: Remove it.

Victor takes his moustache off.

> RAY: We'll try it like that.

> VICTOR: With it?

> RAY: Without it . . . You don't mind?

> VICTOR: Not at all. (*Both laugh heartily.*)

Soumendu Roy at left gives instructions, as camera pans from left to right, bringing the piano into prominent view, and another member of the crew, facing the open window at right of frame, checks on the light.

> SOUMENDU ROY: Put on the lights outside . . . the lights outside . . . The wall this side.

The lights come up.

Soumendu Roy tests the lights.

SOUMENDU ROY: Let it be. It's OK.

Ray in medium shot with his crew, and Soumitra Chatterjee, discussing details (unintelligible).

RAY: . . . So it won't be there?

The crew carry the camera to position and set it up.

Credits again.

CREDITS: SOUND: HITENDRA GHOSH

RAY (off): When you take the full shots then.

Ray sits down beside the camera on a low seat, as the camera pans from left to right to bring the piano into view, with the crew checking on its details, the score sheet in its place, etc.

VOICE (off): Get me two clips please from Dilip.

Ray in medium close shot, pipe in mouth, beside camera, looking into it, calling for Soumendu Roy, who comes into frame, leaning over him.

RAY: Shouldn't we go for 35 for the two-shot? For the pull-back? Without some depth it would be awful.

SOUMENDU ROY: I'm doing just that.

RAY: So you're doing that? Right. (*Nods in satisfaction.*)

Credits again.

CREDITS: CAMERA: GOVIND NIHALANI

RAY (off): That's all. That's the shot.

Ray frames the shot with his hands before guiding Swatilekha, playing Bimala, to her place beside the piano before the open window. Back to camera, he takes Swatilekha's satchel from her hands, and keeps it aside, as she says, 'The script's there.' Ray holds a book in his hand and stands in the position Swatilekha will eventually take.

RAY: Switch off the fan . . . Is this the right position, Roy?

Swatilekha stands beside him, both facing camera, till a member of the crew comes up and confirms. Ray hands the book over to Swatilekha who takes her position, book in hand. Ray turns to left, then faces camera, and calls out.

RAY: Jennifer, take your position at the piano (*he pronounces 'piano' with a funny accent*), and fake.

Jennifer comes into frame and sits at the piano, as Ray leaves frame at left.

RAY (*off*): We'll do a rehearsal.

Ray looks through the camera before crossing over to Swatilekha at right of frame to give her instructions while Jennifer sits waiting at the piano. Soumendu Roy and other members of the crew go on making last minute arrangements, with the camera following them all through, till Ray stops at the centre of the frame for a while, brooding. The camera shifts to Swatilekha and Jennifer sharing some unintelligible joke before Swati comes into a medium close view.

RAY: Babu!

Jennifer, left of frame, at piano, humming the song, with the voices of the crew in the background. Camera pans to the right to concentrate on Swatilekha, who now joins in the singing.

SONG: Let me forget that so long you have rov'd,
　　　　Let me believe that you love as you lov'd,
　　　　Long long ago, long ago . . .

Ray, in close-up, gets ready to take the shot, picking his teeth, before settling down to the camera, and looking through.

> RAY: OK, ready. Can we have a rehearsal please? One rehearsal please.

Jennifer at piano, right of frame, with Swati at centre behind the piano, book in hand.

> JENNIFER (*singing*): Sing me the songs I delighted to hear.

Close-up of camera, bringing Ray into prominence behind it, as camera moves, and Ray peers beyond his camera to draw Jennifer's attention and addresses her.

> RAY: The last time was fine. Let's try it. It was duped. Are you actually reading the book?
>
> JENNIFER: No.
>
> RAY: You got it all by heart?
>
> JENNIFER: All of it.
>
> RAY: I want you to cheat your look a bit towards the left. OK?
>
> JENNIFER: Yes.

Ray at the camera. Camera pans to right to hold the actual shot— Miss Gilby (Jennifer) at the piano giving Bimala (Swatilekha) her singing lessons, Jennifer seen in profile, over the shoulder.

> JENNIFER (*singing*): Sing me the songs I delighted to hear,
>   Long long ago, long ago.

The shot ends with a member of the crew holding a light meter close to Swati's face.

Soumitra Chatterjee and a visitor on the set, seen talking among themselves.

SOUMITRA: I don't remember the name . . .

RAY (*off*): Hey, two of you, will you stand there?

SOUMITRA: It's Andrew. Andrew . . . something.

VOICE (*off*): Silence.

Camera close behind Ray's camera catches Jennifer and Swatilekha at the piano, with a bearded clapper giving the clap: 1/1 Take 1.

RAY: Action.

Long shot of the scene, as Jennifer plays at the piano for some time, before breaking into song, with the crew spread all over the area at a safe distance.

JENNIFER (*singing*): Tell me the tales that to me were so dear,
Long long ago, long ago.

Swatilekha repeats, as camera pans to left, with a glimpse of someone keeping the rhythm with his hands, back to the camera.

Medium close shot, from low angle, of Ray at his camera, under a black cloth, his striped shirt barely visible under it, as Ray shoots the singing lesson scene, with Jennifer singing at the piano, Swatilekha repeating the song with her. The shot closes on camera panning away at right.

JENNIFER (*singing*): Sing me the songs I delighted to hear,
Long long ago, long ago.
Now you have come, all my grief is removed,
Let me forget that so long you have rov'd,
Let me believe that you love as you lov'd
Long long ago, long ago . . .

Last credits.

DIRECTION: SHYAM BENEGAL

Ray takes off the black cloth, with a 'Cut'.

Ray appears in view again, the camera panning left to right, and back to left again, with the crew and Soumitra Chatterjee clapping, as Ray speaks.

RAY: Perfect.

Swatilekha and Jennifer can be seen from over the shoulders of the rest of the crew.

Medium close shot of Ray at left of frame, script in hand, coaching Jennifer, made up as Miss Gilby. Victor Banerjee, dressed as Nikhil, is also in the shot, listening to Ray intently.

RAY (*to Jennifer*): That will be your cue . . . 'Good morning, Mr Choudhuri'. (*To Victor*) 'Good morning. How is your pupil doing?'

Jennifer obviously points to a discrepancy in Ray's own script. Ray takes his pen out to correct it.

RAY: Yes, indeed. Isn't that in your script?

JENNIFER: No.

RAY: Where does it come?

JENNIFER: Right at the beginning, after 'Good morning'

Victor and Jennifer in conversation, their voices, indistinct, continuing on to the next shot.

Close-up of Ray's shooting script, with his own sketches all over. The camera moves along his hand to catch his profile as he corrects with a smile. Jennifer and Victor in the meantime rehearse their parts.

JENNIFER: And history, and geography. Her grammar is improving a lot.

RAY: Geography?

JENNIFER: No, her history, her grammar.

She bursts into laughter as she says this. Ray and Victor, off-screen, join her. She continues.

JENNIFER: Her grammar is improving so much. She wrote a very good essay about birds.

RAY (*off*): Great.

Ray comes into view, coaching Victor through his lines.

RAY: I think she can sing too.

VICTOR: Oh, yes.

The same drawing room setting in long shot, with the light filtering through the lace curtains of a big window, the piano standing against a wall. Jennifer sits at one end of a period sofa with green velvet upholstery. She is ready for another shot, with a bandage wrapped around her temple. Victor as Nikhilesh stands behind the sofa at the extreme right of the frame. Ray is on the floor, half reclining, at left of frame, giving directions to the artistes from the position where the camera will be placed later. Soumendu Roy is seen kneeling just behind him, looking at the artistes. Victor is obviously refreshing Jennifer's memory with the help of a piece of paper held in his hand.

VICTOR: I was on my way back from Church and on the way home . . .

RAY (*pointing his finger to Victor*): You have your dialogues which are the latest version?

JENNIFER: The right one?

RAY: The right one.

VICTOR (*to Jennifer*): Want a look at it?

JENNIFER: No.

The same set-up from a closer distance, with Ray looking at his art-istes rehearsing, through his fingers in front of his eyes forming a lens. Soumendu Roy kneels, looking at them from the same height as Ray.

JENNIFER: That's all I'll say.

RAY: Oh, that's it. You will be looking this way.

He gestures with his hand to indicate the direction he would like Jennifer to look while she spoke.

JENNIFER: Yes.

With that she goes back to speaking her lines.

JENNIFER: That they should do this to me.

VICTOR: Then I'll say, 'They are doing some very stupid things these days, Miss Gilby.'

JENNIFER: No . . . What?

There is some confusion apparently, and Jennifer, looking for clarifi-cation, takes the piece of paper from Victor's hand. As she looks at it:

RAY (*off*): They are doing very stupid things.

VICTOR: You've gone back there?

JENNIFER: No . . . Sorry, yes.

The same set-up seen from a different angle this time, with Victor and Jennifer, their profiles to the camera, and Ray, still peering at them through his framing fingers, from left of the frame. He dis-cusses something with Soumendu Roy in a low voice so as not to disturb the rehearsal that goes on.

JENNIFER (*rehearsing*): One of them picked up a stone. Oh, it was too dreadful.

VICTOR: They are doing some very stupid things, Miss Gilby. I don't blame the boys as much as I blame some of our politi-cal leaders . . . Was that right?

JENNIFER: Yes.

VICTOR: Yes, that's it.

Ray, in mid-close shot, sits on the floor at left of frame, chewing a paan, as he waits for the camera to be placed for him. As the crew set up the camera, the handle of the camera comes uncomfortably close to him. He moves it away and asks the boys to place it a little higher. Ananta Das, the make-up man, has in the meantime come forward to put blood marks on Miss Gilby for the final shooting.

ANANTA (*off*): Manik-da!

RAY (*to the crew setting up the camera*): Lift it up, lift it up. (*To Ananta, putting stains on Jennifer's dress*) Where are you putting it?

ANANTA: Here.

RAY: No, a little higher . . . I can't see.

JENNIFER: It's all sliding down. Hey, be quick!

RAY: It won't stay that way. Yes, yes, smear that way, or it won't stay.

Ray, in close-up, gets ready to take the shot, peering through the lens. Camera pans from Ray to a member of the crew helping with the camera, then to Jennifer and Victor in the same position as they were rehearsing in, and pans back to Ray, watching them intently, till he decides to elevate the chairs a little. Jennifer's voice is heard, off-screen, faintly.

RAY: We have to do something about the chair, it has to be lifted up a little.

SOUMENDU ROY (*off*): I'll put four . . .

RAY (*interrupting him*): Or the camera will have to be lowered . . .

SOUMENDU ROY (*off*): No, that can't be done.

Soumendu Roy, standing beside Ray, passes the instructions on to his crew.

SOUMENDU ROY: Hey, have you brought the four bricks?

As Jennifer and Swatilekha sit side by side on the sofa, Ray, with his back to camera, bends over Swatilekha to give her a few last minute instructions. He rearranges with a touch the end of the sari on her head before turning around to call Victor for the shot. One of the assistants stands between the two women, checking the light with his light meter. A photographer, back to camera, takes stills.

RAY (*to Swatilekha*): You'll speak your dialogues, looking to this side. OK?

SWATILEKHA: OK.

RAY (*calling*): Victor!

AN ASSISTANT (*calling out to the crew*): Lower the lights a little . . .

Quite a crowd of visitors watch the shooting. There are photographers too with their cameras. Soumitra Chatterjee, who plays Sandip in the film, *Ghare Bairey*, is among them, without make-up. The camera shifts from them, across the drawing room lavishly decorated with period furniture, to Jennifer on the sofa with green velvet upholstery, and Victor standing behind her, before focusing on Ray, half reclining, the camera in front of him, and the members of the crew around him. There is a mild argument as to the position of the camera.

Soumitra Chatterjee, seated in an antique chair, smoking a pipe, a part of the designed marble floor visible behind him, as he watches, totally absorbed, the preparations for the shot.

Long shot of the drawing-room set-up, as members of the crew move off the floor. Swatilekha and Jennifer sit on the sofa. Ray's wife, Mrs Bijaya Ray, makes a few adjustments to Swatilekha's costume before moving off.

AN ASSISTANT (*shouting*): Lights on.

RAY (*off*): Let's have a look at you.

The camera at last in position, Ray peers through the lens, his hand on the handle. At the sound of a voice calling someone, he quietly says: 'Silence!' The assistant covers his head with the black sheet.

Two pairs of feet, Miss Gilby's and Bimala's, rest on two cane stools, obviously below the sightline of the camera. Camera begins at the feet, then rises to the two women sitting side by side on the sofa, Bimala, solemn, and Miss Gilby, upset and weeping. Nikhilesh stands behind his wife, behind him an ornate wall bracket. An assistant stands before the window, holding up a piece of glass, obviously to diffuse the direct light.

JENNIFER–MISS GILBY: Such a shock, Mr Choudhuri, to think they should do this to me.

VICTOR–NIKHILESH: Schoolboys, were they, Miss Gilby?

JENNIFER–MISS GILBY: I know their faces. They used to smile at me, greet me.

A top shot of the whole set-up, with the characters at the centre, the piano, a chest of drawers, a marble-top table and the sofa adding up to create the environment. Ray, at extreme left, covered by the black cloth and surrounded by his crew, is busy shooting. The microphone on a boom hangs out of the range of Ray's camera, close to the artistes. Camera slowly zooms back to cover a bigger area of the shooting floor, as Jennifer continues as Miss Gilby.

JENNIFER–MISS GILBY: And now today, I don't know what came over them. I'd been to Church, and on the way back, I passed them, standing outside the grocery store. I smiled at them, and then one of them picked up a stone. Oh!

Close-up of Ray shooting, still under the black cloth, with a member of the crew standing behind him, and a view of hands, other men's, helping with the camera.

JENNIFER–MISS GILBY: It was too dreadful.

Another top shot of the shooting in progress, with the camera slowly zooming in.

VICTOR–NIKHILESH: They're doing some very stupid things these days, Miss Gilby. I don't blame our boys so much as I blame some of our politicians.

JENNIFER–MISS GILBY: It's not SO much the pain, Mr Choudhuri, it's the shock. I don't know what to do now, I can't stay here after this. I'd be sorry to leave. You've been so good to me . . . you and Bimala.

RAY: Cut.

As the crew standing beside him switch off the camera, Ray throws off the black sheet covering him.

RAY: Fine. That is the best unquestionably.

The boom with the hanging mike is carefully removed.

A clip from *Sadgati* (*Deliverance*), with Dukhi (Om Puri), a bundle of grass on his head, and Jhuria (Smita Patil), his wife. He instructs her as to what she should purchase to appease the brahman who was expected to come to their house for the engagement of their daughter. As they walk along, the camera slowly zooms back to reveal that the film is being screened for dubbing, with Ray watching, his back to camera.

DUKHI: A pound of flour.

JHURIA: A pound of flour.

DUKHI: A half of rice. Repeat.

JHURIA: A half of rice.

DUKHI: A quarter of gram.

JHURIA (*dutifully*): A quarter of gram.

DUKHI: An eighth of ghee.

JHURIA: An eighth of ghee.

DUKHI: Salt and turmeric.

Smita Patil and Om Puri watching the screening, now off-screen; Ray stands behind them pipe in mouth, watching intently. As they watch, Om Puri starts repeating the lines, Smita laughs and joins in. Camera dollies round to face them, as they repeat the lines, rehearsing for the dubbing, till Ray taps Smita on the shoulder to remind her not to slap her forehead as she had done in the film. The camera slowly zooms closer to focus on Ray standing at the centre, his right hand holding a pipe to his mouth, as Smita and Om repeat their lines for the dubbing, out of focus. As they finish, Ray nods his approval and they turn back, laughing.

Ray, with his back to the camera, watches the piece from *Sadgati* on the screen, where Dukhi and Jhuria approach the camera.

DUKHI: A pound of flour, a half of rice.

In the projection room, a row of empty seats, with Ray seated in one, pipe in mouth. Smita stands closer to the camera, out of focus. She turns to Ray as he speaks to her.

RAY: Smita, don't do that slapping, because it has been done with the bangles already. There is the sound of your bangles.

Close-up of Ray's profile, seated alone in the same seat, watching intently as the dubbing goes on. Off-screen there is the sound of Smita bursting into uncontrollable sobbing.

The weeping continues as Smita, left of frame, holds the end of her sari to her mouth and sobs. Ray watches from his seat at a distance, at the edge of his seat with tension.

RAY: Cut.

As he says this, he relaxes into his seat. Smita, too, stops weeping and puts the edge of her sari down from her mouth.

Recording in progress. Ray in close-up, seen in profile, frowns in concentration, as he listens to the voices of Smita and Om, off-screen. Ray bends over to speak to one of the recordists, in an inaudible whisper. Then they again listen intently.

Another film clip from *Sadgati*. A pair of stiff legs, obviously of a dead man, cover the frame, till a hand lifts one of the legs with the help of a crooked staff. The other hand slips in a knot around the ankle dextrously, scrupulously avoiding touching the dead man. Once the knot is secure around the ankle, there is a tug at the rope.

The brahman (played by Mohan Agashe), his sacred thread around his right ear, as is customary while doing a job considered unclean, stands against the fading light of the sky. As he gets a strong grip on the rope, he turns his back to the camera, ready now to lug the body across the fields to its destination.

The dead man (played by Om Puri), legs first, then the torso, and finally the head, is tugged across the frame along the ground. Against a darkening sky, the brahman passes, dragging his burden with an effort, from left to right of frame, with only his head and shoulders visible.

The brahman, in silhouette, panting under the weight of the dead man, passes across the cloudy sky, as the drums start beating in the background.

The ankle, held in the knot of the rope, passes in silhouette from left to right of frame. The sky gets darker to the beating of the drums.

A low angle shot of the brahman's back, with his sacred thread and the rope tied to the dead man's ankle crossing each other, as the drums beat.

The body is pulled across a bush from left to right of frame. The drums beat.

In a long shot, the brahman pulls the body across an embankment, to the beating of the drums.

A low angle shot of the brahman against the sky, changing shoulders, as he cannot bear it on one shoulder any longer. The drums beat.

A low angle long shot shows the brahman against the darkening sky, coming towards the camera, bent with exhaustion. He slips and almost falls once, from the strain. The body, its limbs grotesquely turning at the joints, follows him.

The dead body has been dumped in what the camera reveals, as it zooms slowly back, to be a dumping ground of animal bones and skulls.

The film clip ends to bring Ray into view, relaxing in a comfortable chair, one leg above the knee of the other, with a bookcase behind him, and an open window at left, both only partly visible. So is Shyam

Benegal himself, back to camera, interviewing Ray. Ray is dressed in an off-white kurta and white pyjamas, sandals, and a shawl wrapped around him. The camera zooms to him slowly as he speaks.

> RAY: I was born in a place called Gadpar Road, in a printing press actually. In fact, it was a huge building which housed the printing and blockmaking departments which my grandfather had started, called U. Roy and Sons.

Camera pans over a part of the road and its old buildings, now all discoloured with age and showing the ravages of time and neglect till it finally stops before a building, obviously the house Ray is talking about. It must have had an impressive facade once, now totally out of repair, with a tree flourishing out of its red-brick wall against the sky.

> RAY: I was born there in 1921, and I spent the first six years of my life in that place.

Camera pans from right to left over the balcony of the building, as Ray continues his reminiscences.

> RAY: I think the most vivid memory is of the printing press and blockmaking department because I used to spend my afternoons there . . .

A clip from *Aparajito* (*The Unvanquished*), showing Apu working at a treadle press.

> RAY (*off*): . . . the department of the compositors and I would just walk in . . .

Apu works behind the treadle with another worker at right of frame helping him learn his job.

RAY (*off*): . . . and there was the process camera which used to fascinate me a great deal. Then I would take little drawings with me . . .

Mix to a close-up of Apu, still working at the treadle. He wipes off his sweat with the edge of his shirt and looks up sideways, obviously to the wall clock on which it is already past ten at night.

RAY (*off*): . . . doodles, and tell the blockmaking department chaps to make a block of them for the *Sandesh*.

A clip from yet another Ray film—*Charulata*. Bhupati sits dejectedly in a chair in his press, with open shelves loaded with books and papers all around. Amal stands behind him at a little distance, his head bent, his face thoughtful. With a sigh, Bhupati stands up, turns round with his walking stick in his hand and faces Amal. He puts a hand on Amal's shoulder, who looks away. The pendulum of the wall clock swings, marking time.

RAY: They would always say, yes, it will come out next month, but they never did. That really is the dominant memory, and the smell of turpentine which I had forgotten, but I smelt it again when I went to a press when I was in advertising, and immediately all the memories of Gadpar came rushing back.

As Ray's voice trails off, the background music and the dialogue in the film clip surface.

BHUPATI: A very favourite smell of mine—the smell of printing ink. Come, let's go.

As Bhupati and Amal, in the film clip, move towards the door, Ray's voice resumes over the shot, and continues to the next shot, which again focuses on the balcony of the ancestral house, this time from a different angle.

> RAY: I didn't actually have any brothers or cousins or anything, but there was a servant's son . . . They used to fly the kite . . .

A sequence from *Shatranj ke Khiladi* (*The Chess Players*), showing kites in the sky, crowds of excited young and old men on ground flying them, and then again the kites flying in the sky.

> RAY (*off*): . . . every afternoon from the roof and we have this puja, you know, the Vishwakarma, on which particular day the sky is just full of kites.

Ray, in close-up, wrapped in the white shawl, against a bookcase behind him.

> RAY: I never saw my grandfather because he died five or six years before I was born and my father fell ill almost about the same time that I was born, and he was in bed most of the time for about two and a half years. He had Kala-azar, and he died in 1923.

The camera slowly zooms from inside a dimly lit room across an old-fashioned cross-grilled window to focus on a sunlit courtyard outside. A newborn baby's cry is heard from somewhere.

> RAY (*off*): I was two and a half then. Another three years I think we stayed in Gadpar Road in north Calcutta.

A long shot of the old ancestral home of the Rays.

> RAY (*off*): Then the business folded up for reasons which I never found out.

Ray, in close-up, in his room.

> RAY: My mother and I moved to my maternal uncle's house . . .

From across a road along which cars and pedestrians cross incessantly the camera closes in to a well maintained old house with an impressive porch in front. A turret-like balustrade on the terrace flaunts a present-day TV antenna jutting out—obviously a view of the house as it stands now.

> RAY: . . . towards south Calcutta, Bhawanipur. I—my mother
> and I were staying there. I remember her as working.

A film clip from *Charulata*. Charu's hand embroiders a design on a piece of cloth stretched out on a frame, with the letter 'B' as the centre piece of the design: 'B' is the first letter of her husband's name, Bhupati.

> RAY (*off*): She was a very hard worker. She used to do embroidery,
> clay modelling . . .

A film clip from *Aparajito* shows Sarbajaya, sitting with her back to camera, obviously mending something with great concentration. Apu, back home on a holiday, is reading a book by the light of a lantern that stands at one side the bed, its mattress rolled to one side and a mosquito net hanging against the wall. It is a poor woman's room, with nothing in excess of the bare minimum. Mother and son carry on a conversation in the background, with Ray's voice coming over.

> RAY: . . . drawings, and sewing, and leatherwork also she had
> learnt at one time. She used to keep herself busy, and in the
> afternoons I would be watching her always working, doing
> this and that and all kinds of things, and I did a lot of sketch-
> ing also at that time. I was studying at home. My mother
> taught me whatever I had to learn, and I was very close to

my mother, this much I can remember. She taught me history, geography, arithmetic, English and Bengali, in the early days, but she was very particular that I should be sent to a good school . . .

Close-up of Sarbajaya the mother, in the clip from *Aparajito*, smilingly asking Apu about Calcutta where he studies and works.

> RAY (*off*): . . . and eventually to a good college so I had the best of education.

Close-up of Apu, replying to his mother with a mischievous smile.

> RAY (*off*): She herself took a job later . . .

Close-up of Sarbajaya.

> RAY (*off*): . . . in a widows' home, and she was teaching, and we used to spend holidays . . .

In a low angle shot from *Kanchenjunga*, a band plays bagpipes on the Mall in Darjeeling.

> RAY (*off*): . . . very exciting holidays in hill stations in Bihar, and we spent a long holiday . . .

In a long shot, in the film clip, Manisha (Aloknanda Roy), walks towards the Mall, crossing a fountain in the foreground.

> RAY (*off*): . . . in Darjeeling . . . and the . . .

The back of Chaudhuri's (Chhabi Biswas) head visible against a glorious sunset in Darjeeling. As Chaudhuri slowly turns to look for his family and walks across the frame, leaving it at one point, the blurred snow peaks of the great Kanchenjunga, golden in the rays of the setting sun, come into focus and fill the frame.

RAY (*off*): . . . the first sight of Kanchenjunga was really just unforgettable, that I remember very, very well. At six o'clock in the morning my mother woke me up and said, Come and have a look, and I stood at the window, and there were the snows, red, pink, with the sunlight, with the snow catching the sunlight.

In a film clip from *Charulata*, the Bay of Bengal stretches to the horizon, with Bhupati standing in mid-long shot on the sands, with his back to the sea. He throws up his hands in delight and runs forward to where Charulata sits leaning against a sandbank, with her back to camera. As Bhupati kneels down before her, the camera dollies round to bring Charu into focus, listening to her husband's exuberance, as he gesticulates with his left hand in which he holds his pipe.

RAY (*off*): . . . and the first sight of the sea at Puri was very exciting also. So these are the memories that come back to me and then my uncle's . . .

An old motor car with a convertible top comes from a distance along a quiet road skirting the old race course in Calcutta, in a clip from *Parashpathar* (*The Philosopher's Stone*). As it passes in front of the camera and moves to the right, the camera follows its movement.

RAY (*off*): . . . first motor car, then our trip to the maidan every afternoon . . .

The camera follows in the same pace as in the previous shot a station wagon, which passes the old car, now at a halt. As the camera comes to a stop, the Victoria Memorial comes into view in the background, seen hazily against the sky.

RAY (*off*): . . . and around the Victoria Memorial, and then at the age of nine I started going to school.

Through the serrated leaves of a palm tree, the sloping roof and tile-topped porch of an old-fashioned brick building come into view, with a grass-covered patch of land before it.

>RAY (*off*): It was called the Ballygunge Government High School. Did turn out to be a very good school. It would be 1930 when I joined school . . .

An arched entrance at the end of a long corridor gleaming in bright sunlight, in a long shot, with the camera in a wide circular movement sweeping across the sunlit ground outside, till it stops at the other end of the same corridor.

>RAY (*off*): . . . and I was interested in games—quite a bit more as an observer. I was very interested in football and cricket . . .

A black and white photograph, probably a newspaper clipping, showing Ray's uncle, Saradaranjan Ray, with the camera moving upwards from his pad-covered legs and cricket bat to his bearded face, partly shadowed by the hat he wears.

>RAY (*off*): . . . and there were cricketers in the family. The leading Bengali cricketer was an uncle of mine.

Close-up of Ray, wrapped in the white shawl, speaking of his ancestors.

>RAY: Even before my grandfather brought out his children's magazine, he had done abridgements for children of the Mahabharata and the Ramayana, and another collection of stories from the Mahabharata, which do not directly relate to the Pandavas and the Kauravas.

A sequence of illustrations done by Upendrakishore Ray Choudhury—a boat setting sail; a rider, scared and uncomfortable on a crocodile; a pack of battling demons. As Ray speaks, a musical piece from *Goopy Gyne* breaks upon the scene.

> RAY: You know that there are lots of stories within stories and they were already very famous. They were among the first abridgements for children and they have not been improved upon since.

The famous sequence of the dance of the ghosts from Ray's *Goopy Gyne Bagha Byne*, made from a story by his grandfather. The camera slowly zooms back from the close shot against the music continuing from the previous shot.

Close shot of Ray.

> RAY: And he was quite close to the Tagore family because they had the same kind of activities. In fact the Tagores had brought out one of the first children's magazines long before *Sandesh*, and he was writing for that also, and he was a friend of . . .

The camera slowly zooms towards a typical wash painting by Abanindranath Tagore.

> RAY: . . . Abanindranath who was a painter, because there was this common interest . . .

The camera moves upwards from the feet of a portrait of Rabindranath Tagore done in the same wash style.

> RAY: . . . and Rabindranath who was about the same age as my grandfather. They were very close to each other particularly because . . .

A black and white portrait of Upendrakishore playing the violin.

> RAY (*off*): My grandfather would often go to Tagore's house in Jorasanko in Calcutta to play the violin during the Magh Festival of the Brahmos.

Camera broods over beautifully panelled glass doors, with stained glass side panels and arches. As Ray speaks, a song breaks in, subdued, with the grainy timbre of an old record.

> RAY (*off*): They have the Maghotsava as it is called, and he was needed to play the violin along with the chorus and the solos. So he was very close to them.

Ray in close shot.

> RAY: But around 1912–13 he felt that he had to bring out his own magazine. By that time the printing press was well established and you can see from the first year or two of *Sandesh* . . .

Blow-up of a *Sandesh* cover.

> RAY (*off*): . . . that the quality of printing was extraordinarily high.

A side profile, slightly from the back, of Upendrakishore, working at a typewriter—or is it a typesetting machine?

> RAY (*off*): But soon after that my grandfather died, and my father took over.

Ray in close-up.

> RAY: He was also a very extraordinary writer and illustrator.

A sequence of illustrations done by Sukumar Ray, Ray's father, for his own books, especially *HaJaBaRaLa* and *Abol Tabol*, including those for the poems 'Khudor Kal', 'Kumdo Patash', 'Budir Badi', 'Kimbhut', 'Bhutudey Khela', 'Note Boi', 'Bhoy Peyo Na', 'Tansh Goru', 'Paloan' and a sketch of Hiji-Bij-Bij, the inveterate laugher in 'HaJaBaRaLa'.

> RAY (*off*): He was not as professional as my grandfather, but he had certain unique qualities, like the drawings he did for his nonsense rhymes or the funny stories that he wrote. He had an absolutely unique style of doing comic illustrations which nobody else has shown in India.

A clipping from Ray's *Goopy Gyne Bagha Byne*, beginning with a close-up of the King of the Ghosts.

> THE KING: I am the king, the king of ghosts,
> I give three gifts
> If I am pleased.

Goopy and Bagha laugh in wild glee, clap their hands and cry out.

> GOOPY AND BAGHA: Three gifts.

A sequence of six photographs from Ray's childhood, with an old record of a Tagore song sung by Kanak Das, his aunt, playing faintly in the background.

> RAY: I remember songs and singing a great deal, because my mother used to sing very well and my aunt was quite a ccl-ebrated singer. She used to . . .

Ray as a young man, with his mother.

> RAY: . . . make records for HMV and I remember very vividly . . .

A sequence of seven shots in black and white, beginning with the show windows of some of the famous shops of yesteryears selling gramophone records, with their names appearing in clear, bold letters: New Gramophone Stores and Harry's Music House; followed by photographs of the interior of the Gramophone Company in Calcutta, with European and Indian workers: a recording session in one of the studios; the HMV dog bringing the series to a close: with the Kanak Das song continuing in the background.

> RAY: . . . my trips to the HMV, the Gramophone Company studios, and the first recording session which I attended. I think I was about six and a half or seven at that time. That was before the electrical recording days. They used to have to sing in front of a horn. And they were all English engineers and that I remember very well.

Close-up of Ray, talking animatedly.

> RAY: For some mysterious reason there were some records of classical music in our house although nobody was really interested, Western Classical music. There was one movement of Beethoven's violin concerto.

A sequence of gramophone discs displaying their labels—all of them Western Classical numbers, in Columbia and HMV releases.

> RAY: They were the usual things, which I think even the Bengalis bought then, violin records by Chrysler, songs by Chaliapin, and things like that. Every sort of well-to-do or upper class Bengali or middle class house had some records of Western music. Violin was very popular as an instrument, so there would be records of Chrysler playing odd pieces.

Ray in close-up.

RAY: Sketching, painting, drawing, I had it at the back of my mind . . .

A sequence of three sketches made by Ray at an early period of his life.

RAY (*off*): . . . while I was in college or even high school, that I would be a professional artist doing perhaps some kind of commercial art, but I had no training for that.

A long top shot of College Street, the heart of the city's University district, with the camera panning to a side view of the impressive Victorian building of Presidency College, one of Calcutta's oldest colleges.

RAY (*off*): When the time came for me to decide what subjects I shall specialize in, I had a very close friend of my father's who was a statistician, Professor Mahalanobis, you may have heard of him, and he said, 'You should study economics . . .'

The camera takes a closer look at the college building, recording the name—Presidency College—written on top of an arch, and then slowly zooms back to reveal the full facade with its impressive gothic pillars.

RAY (*off*): ' . . . because I have a magazine, a statistical magazine called *Sankhya*. You can always get a job there for two hundred and fifty rupees a month or something.' I was not terribly interested in economics really, and I think my two years as a student of the BA class was more or less wasted.

A present-day view of the college, with students passing from the left to the right of the frame, with their backs to the camera, which tilts up to take in a few treetops and part of the facade of the building, with the pillars supporting the arch, the name of the college in large capital letters over the arch, and finally the watch tower.

> RAY (*off*): *I* lost interest in college, because it was not really for me. I had to study, I passed, I got an honours in economics, but it was not really my subject. But then . . .

Ray, in close-up.

> RAY: . . . my mother suggested, and I also agreed rather readily, that I should go to Santiniketan and spend some time there . . .

A typical Santiniketan scene, a class going on under a tree, in long shot.

> RAY (*off*): . . . and to be . . .

Under a tree, in medium shot, a girl sits sketching from nature, with several students in the distance. The camera pans to two more girls sitting under an ancient tree with a gnarled trunk, sketching.

> RAY (*off*): Tagore was still living and they had some marvellous teachers like Nandalal Bose and Benode Behari Mukherjee, Ramkinkar Baij, and to be there for some time . . .

A sculpture by Ramkinkar, with one of the old Santiniketan houses in the background. The camera zooms back slowly to bring into view the whole house flanked by trees, with a full-throated chorus on the soundtrack.

> RAY (*off*): . . . and she thought it would be a good thing to be in Santiniketan in proximity to Tagore.

The camera zooms closer slowly to a look at a part of one of the houses in which Tagore lived at Santiniketan, with the chorus continuing on the soundtrack.

The same house, in long shot this time, with the typical red soil of the region and bushes of the red bougainvillaea dominating the foreground.

A beautiful alpana design in white on the red soil, with boys and girls adding the finishing touches.

    RAY (*off*): I had some reservations about Indian art.

A sequence of six paintings in the style that Ray describes as Indian art—all in what was also called the wash technique.

    RAY (*off*): The wishy-washy kind of rather sentimental stuff which used to come out in Ramananda Chatterjee's magazines, *Modern Review* and *Prabasi*, at that time. Every month there was a colour reproduction, and I didn't very much care for those, but I found eventually, after joining Santiniketan, that Indian art could also be very strong and virile . . .

Ray, in his chair, talks directly to the camera.

    RAY: . . . and it's not all that sentimental or Victorian kind of stuff.

Another sequence of eight paintings, works by the three Tagores—Rabindranath, Abanindranath, and Gaganendranath—and Nandalal Bose.

    RAY (*off*): I studied painting in Santiniketan but never meant to become a painter. I needed the background of Indian classical art perhaps to be able to . . .

Santal Family, a famous sculpture by Ramkinkar Baij, at Santiniketan.

    RAY (*off*): . . . use it in commercial art later.

Ray, in medium shot, seated as before.

> RAY: So I got to know about Eastern art, Chinese, Japanese, our own schools, and also Western art, I mean, starting from early Egyptian, cave paintings, rock paintings, down to the post-impressionists, or even the later ones.

The camera pans over a long row of pavement bookstalls selling secondhand and rare books on College Street, with people browsing through old books in several of them.

> BENEGAL (*off*): When you came to Calcutta looking for a job did you find it very difficult?

> RAY (*off*): No, actually I found it very easily. It so happened that there was somebody who knew the Assistant Manager of D. J. Keymer and Company who was a Bengali chap, and it turned out that we had known the family.

Camera shifts focus in a long shot from the facade of a severely practical looking building to other buildings, and then to the busy road that is Chittaranjan Avenue, before it zooms slowly closer to the building housing the Central Avenue Coffee House.

> RAY (*off*): I knew his brother, sister; my wife knew the family very well, so this old chap took me to Mr D. K. Gupta, who eventually founded Signet Press, and I began almost as an apprentice, actually a Junior Visualizer.

A sequence of seven covers designed by Ray for the Signet Press, including *Nabaneeta, Sreemati, Jonaki, Dui Badi, Duranta Dupur*, a book of poems by Bishnu De—*Naam Rekhechhi Komal Gandhar*— and Abanindranath Tagore's memoirs—*Apan Katha*.

> RAY (*off*): I was getting sixty-five rupees a month, a dearness allowance of fifteen rupees, and I was learning visualizing

and typography and layouts, and there was a lot of illustration in those days, not like now when you have mostly photographs.

Ray's drawing room, in medium shot, with Shyam Benegal, back to camera, in a deep sofa, and Ray, facing the camera, in another sofa, one leg slung over the other, a bookcase, the window, and his writing table with a lamp on it behind him. As Ray speaks through the shot, the camera slowly zooms closer to him, leaving Benegal out of the frame.

> RAY: Illustrators were actually needed in those days. There was a lot of hand-drawn illustrations, not photography, not models so much. Very few in those days actually.

> BENEGAL (*off*): There was a lot of typographical work done by hand?

> RAY: Also. Yes, yes indeed, because we didn't have a very wide range of types in those days . . .

Two shots of letters and texts in Ray Roman, a typeface that Ray designed.

> RAY (*off*): So that is what I was doing, and I think there was a series which came later.

Three sketches made for advertisements for Paludrine, showing in highly amusing detail the daily life of different sections of the urban society, including the sahibs.

> RAY (*off*): It was a series for Paludrine—enormous ads, just an illustration of various classes of people in Calcutta, the lower middle class, the middle class, even Englishmen. I think there was a series of six advertisements showing in great detail the interior of the houses. The idea was to take

a Paludrine every Sunday morning, so somebody was taking a Paludrine or distributing a Paludrine. There were children around, so that's filmic, very, very filmic. What I was getting slightly fed up with was this having to deal with the clients, you know. Working as, almost as a—you know that was very demeaning.

Ray's profile in close-up.

RAY: Awful! You had very few enlightened clients actually . . . very demeaning, and I was getting—I was really getting very tired of advertising, and I wanted to be absolutely free as an artist.

Ray, in medium shot, facing camera.

RAY: Cinema came of course much later.

A sequence of ten stills of Hollywood stars, including Clark Gable, Greta Garbo, Marlene Dietrich.

RAY (*off*): I think in my early school days my main interest was stars. I was really a film fan and I used to read magazines like *Picturegoer*, *Photoplay*, and *Film Pictorial*, and things like that, but then gradually, I think early in college, I became more and more interested in this directorial aspect of filmmaking. I became aware of the director.

Ray, in close-up.

RAY: And I was reading up on people like John Ford and Ernst Lubitsch, William Wyler and Frank Capra, and looking for their speciality in the film, their sort of special characteristics.

Titles set in
Ray Roman
Typeface designed by
SATYAJIT RAY

FIGURE 1. A credits card from the film, set in Ray Roman,
a typeface designed by Ray.

FIGURE 2. Benegal, Nihalani (with camera) and an assistant,
shooting with Ray in his study.

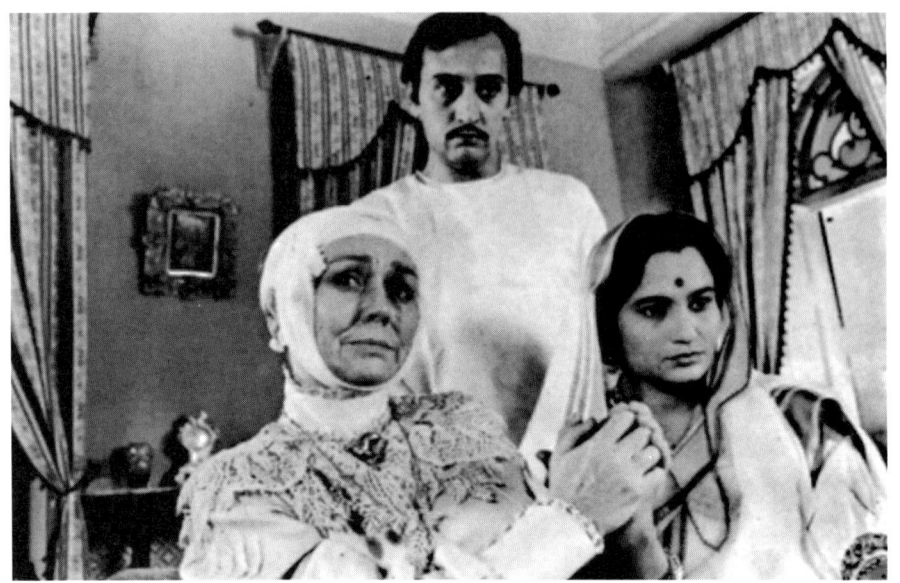

FIGURE 3. A wounded Miss Gilby (Jennifer), Nikhilesh (Victor) and Bimala (Swatilekha) in *Ghare Bairey*.

FIGURE 4. The brahman (Agashe) dragging the dead chamar (Om Puri) to his last resting place, in *Sadgati*.

FIGURES 5-6. The beginning: Ray's first 'treatment' of *Pather Panchali*, illustrating a children's version of the novel: 'it was only [. . .] when I illustrated it that the idea of turning that into a film [. . .] occurred.'

FIGURES 7–10. A page from the *Pather Panchali* scenario: 'I did a book of drawings of the film, of frames [. . .] in wash, black and white, [. . .] and this is what I had, even when I started the film.'

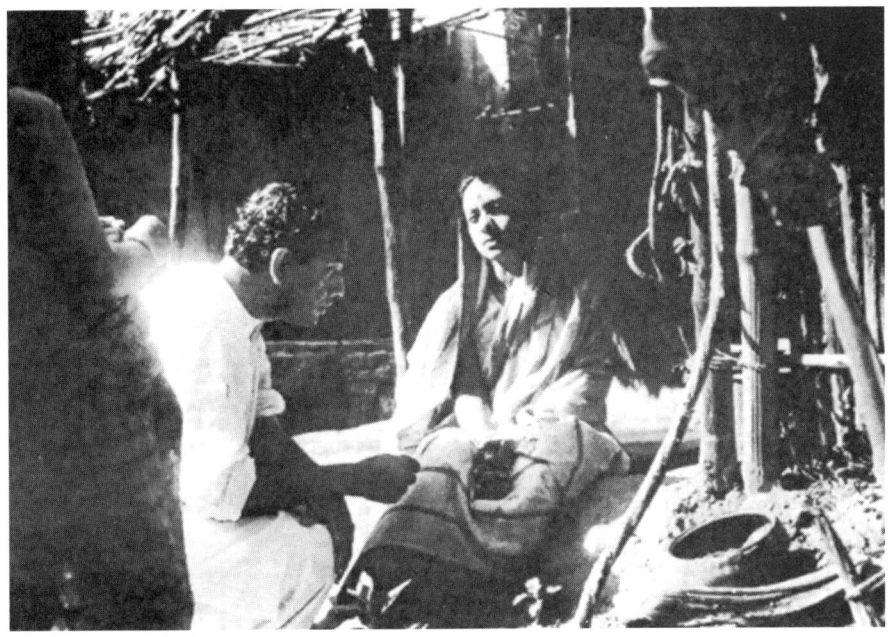

FIGURE 11. Ray briefs Karuna Banerjee for a shot in *Pather Panchali*.

FIGURE 12. Apu, Durga and a scarecrow in a shot from *Pather Panchali*.

FIGURE 13. A scene from *Pather Panchali*: 'even if it was your first film, quite a remarkable control, particularly with the climactic moment when the husband Harihar comes back.'

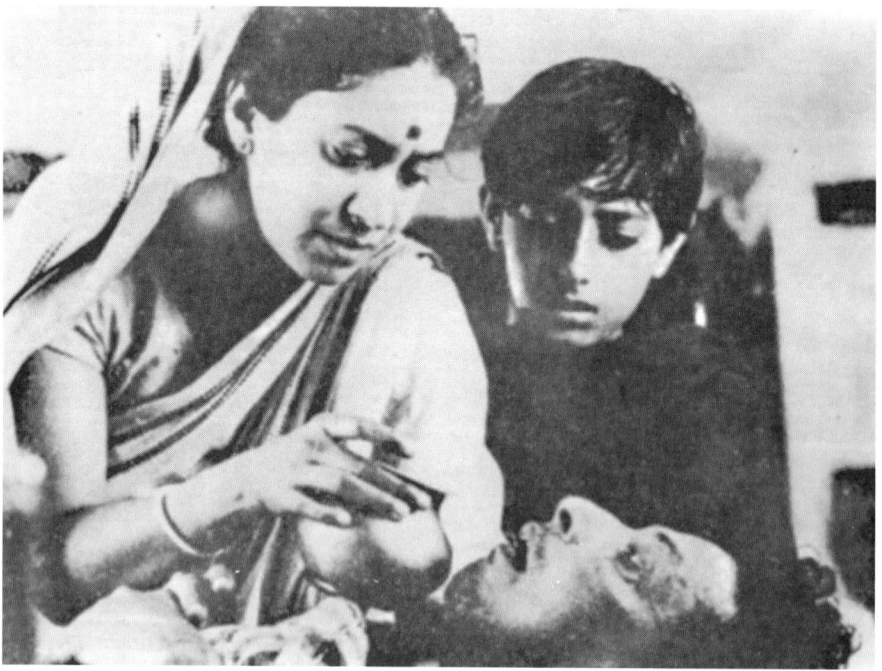

FIGURE 14. The death of Harihar in *Aparajito.*

FIGURE 15. Apu's room, as Ray conceived it for *Apur Sansar*.

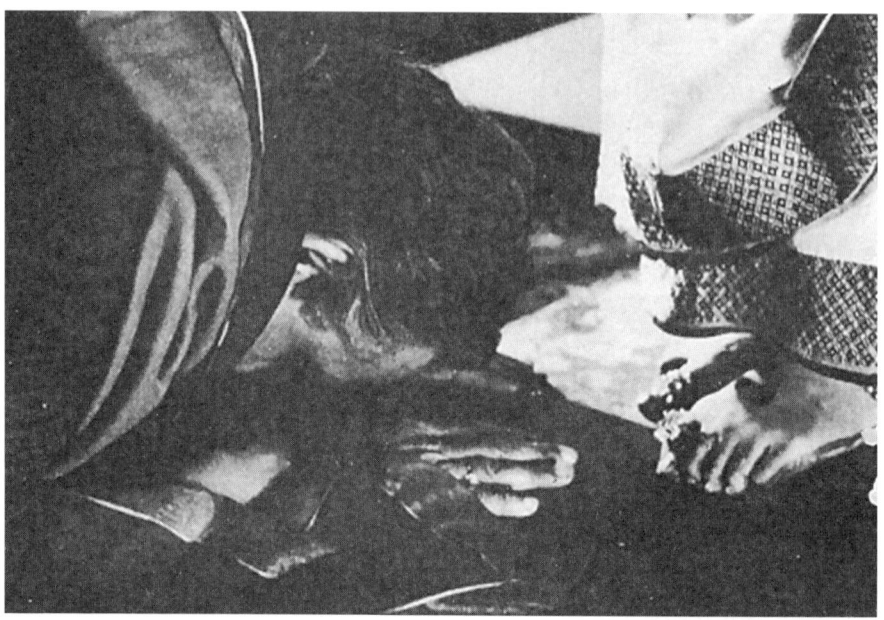

FIGURES 16–17. The authority of superstition: Chhabi Biswas as the father-in-law who believes his daughter-in-law, played by Sharmila Tagore, to be an incarnation of the goddess, in *Devi*.

FIGURES 18–19. Chhabi Biswas as the traditional-decadent patron and Gangapada Bose as the nouveau riche rival admire the dancer played by Roshan Kumari.

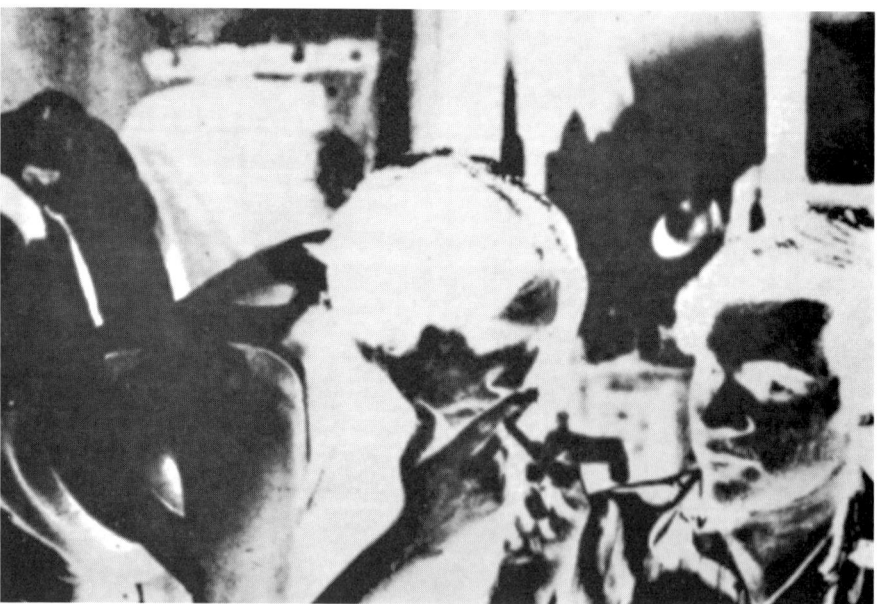

FIGURES 20–21. Siddhartha (Dhritiman), in *Pratidwandi*, faces the selection panel (*top*) and lights the cigarette for the parttime prostitute (*bottom*).

FIGURE 22. Madhabi Chakrabarty as Charu with the opera glasses in *Charulata*.

FIGURE 23. The 'Mozartian' memory game in *Aranyer Dinratri*: 'the game itself is the ground base over which the six characters play out their individual roles in word, look and gesture.'

FIGURE 24. Ray's sketch for Nawab Wajed Ali Shah in *Shatranj ke Khiladi*.

FIGURE 25. The chess players—Meer Roshan Ali (Saeed Jaffrey) and Mirza Sajjad Ali (Sanjeev Kumar)—in *Shatranj ke Khiladi*.

FIGURE 26. The lonely boy, 'drawing white flowers in black', in *Pikoo*.

FIGURE 27. Ray's sketch for *Goopy Gyne Bagha Byne*.

FIGURES 28–29. The dance of the ghosts in *Goopy Gyne Bagha Byne*.

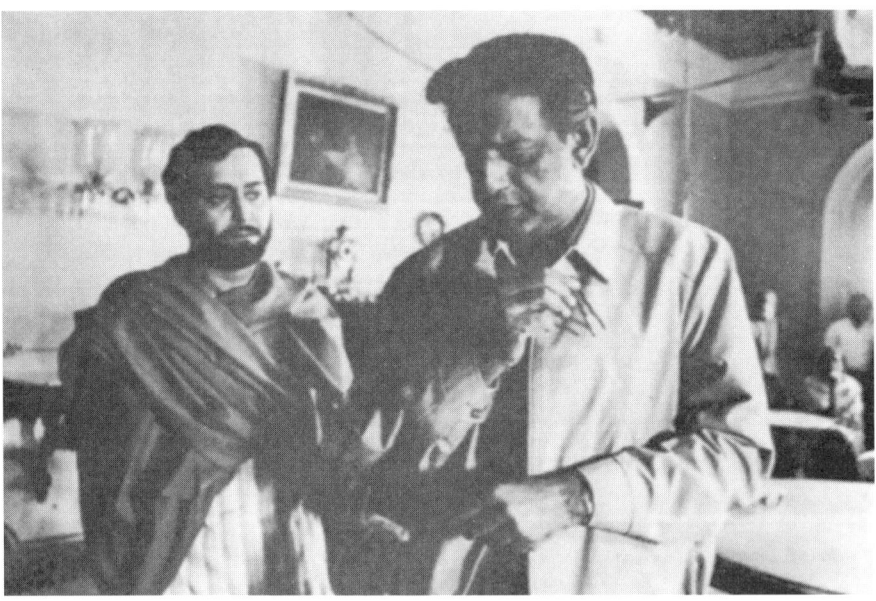

FIGURES 30–31. Soumitra Chatterjee, a favourite of Ray's, as Feluda the detective in *Sonar Kella* (*top*) and as Sandip in *Ghare Bairey* (*bottom*), with Ray on the set.

Ten stills and posters from early Hollywood films by Ford, Capra and others.

> RAY (*off*): *I saw whatever John Ford films I could get to see and then, even later, the early forties or late thirties, Hollywood comedies and the Hollywood thriller, very hard-edged films like the Billy Wilder of the early forties—Double Indemnity, Lost Weekend—and comedies like Major and Minor, Lee McCarey's comedies with Cary Grant and Irene Dunne, which were very fine, and I have re-seen them on Television, and they are still marvellous, and the Frank Capra films of the thirties like It Happened One Night and Mr Smith Goes to Washington and all the others.*

Ray, in close-up.

> RAY: So they were very, very well-crafted films, so my education really is based on these extremely well-written, well-directed, well-shot, well-acted films of the thirties and forties.

A sequence of seven stills from films by Hollywood's European directors.

> RAY: So I got to know the American films made by French directors, who had left France and settled in Hollywood like Duvivier, Renoir himself and a few others, and the Germans like Fritz Lang and others who were making American films—making them in a very German sort of way.

Ray, in close-up.

> RAY: The same goes for the French films, for instance for Renoir's first film that I saw—*The Southerner*.

Close-up in black and white of a man, his head bent to see something through a bush—in a film clip.

> RAY (*off*): It's an American story in an American film made by a French director, acted by Americans, but looking . . .

Cut to close-up of a woman, shocked, in the same place—from the same film.

> RAY (*off*): . . . completely different from the American films. It was more French.

Cut to a close-up of an old man, lying dead.

> RAY (*off*): I mean one could certainly recognize a completely new . . .

The dead man's hand, with a fly hovering over it, and a small, hairy dog lying with its head on the hand. A slow music begins on the soundtrack as Ray's voice continues over the shot.

> RAY (*off*): . . . approach, a narrative approach, a new style of filmmaking . . .

The dog panting, in close-up, with a pair of legs behind him. The slow music on the soundtrack gives way to a thudding sound.

> RAY (*off*): . . . from looking at these American films made by a French director. So when . . .

A roughly hewn wooden cross, bearing the name 'Peter Tucker', with somebody hitting it with a rock in an effort to plant it firmly in the ground.

> RAY (*off*): . . . Renoir came here, I was familiar with his . . .

The man, who had first discovered the dead man, digging in the cross grimly.

    RAY (*off*): . . . French-American films like . . .

A medium shot of a part of a group of mourners, a girl among them with flowers in her hand, praying silently.

    RAY (*off*): . . . *The Southerner*, the various other things he made . . .

The group assembled with the cross in the middle, in medium shot. The man who planted the cross still carries the rock in his right hand, and the small hairy dog is now at his feet, behind the cross. Once the cross is firmly planted, he throws the rock away. The girl places the bouquet at the foot of the cross. The man picks the dog up, takes his hat from someone's hand and puts it on, before starting to walk away as the other mourners come forward to lay flowers on the grave. As the group disperses slowly, the music rises.

    RAY (*off*): . . . *The Diary of a Chambermaid, This Land is Mine.* But I didn't know his French films as yet.

The film clip continues, with the group coming towards the camera, through the fields down a dirt road. At the sound of an approaching car they move aside to the edges of the road allowing two cars and a carriage to pass them by, raising a lot of dust. After the cars are gone, they resume walking down the road.

Ray, in medium close shot, facing camera.

    RAY: But in Santiniketan I was away, cut off from films. I remember that *Citizen Kane* . . .

A *Citizen Kane* poster.

RAY (*off*): . . . came and went in Calcutta and I was away in Santiniketan. It was a great regret that I was not in Calcutta when *Citizen Kane* was shown . . .

Ray, in medium close shot.

RAY: . . . but I made up for the lack of opportunity to see films by reading . . .

Rows of bookcases, in a long shot, with the camera slowly bringing into view a part of Ray's working room, with sunlight streaming in through a window, highlighting Ray's profile as he sits, pipe in mouth, writing something on a piece of paper held to a board resting on his knees.

RAY (*off*): . . . on the cinema as an art form.

Ray, in close-up.

RAY: Nobody thought that cinema was a very secure profession or much good for making money. No, it was not that certainly. I was thinking more in terms of a job as a commercial artist. Films were something to enjoy, not something to make myself. No, there was no question of that at all. In fact that came very much, much much later. Even when we were running the film society . . .

A sequence illustrating early film society publications, with shots of the cover of the first issue of the Calcutta Film Society's news bulletin, a flyleaf with the names of its office bearers, P. C. Mahalanobis the President, Hiran K. Sanyal the Chairman of the Executive Committee, and Satyajit Ray and Chidananda Dasgupta as the joint secretaries; and a page from an article by Ray titled 'Some Italian Films I have seen'.

RAY (*off*): . . . we were anxious to study films, not to make them, but to understand them, that was the situation, and even when the first time I got involved . . .

Ray, in close-up.

RAY: . . . or was about to get involved in a film it was as a script-writer.

Fourteen shots, mixing fast with one another, of a sequence of paintings by Ray of a veena player, the last shot dissolving to a calligraphic 'The End'.

RAY (*off*): You know, one of my hobbies was taking up a story which has been sold for filming to somebody else to do my own treatment and compare it with the treatment on the screen.

Ray, in close-up.

RAY: At one time Jyotirmoy Ray was making a film, and he offered me the job of the art director, which didn't happen eventually. It was Bansi and Subho Tagore who did the art direction for that film, and then when we decided to do Tagore's *Ghare Bairey* I was to be the screenwriter. I had a contract as a screenwriter with a certain producer, and my friend, Hari Sadhan Dasgupta, was supposed to be the director. It was only after I decided on *Pather Panchali* after reading the book when I illustrated it . . .

The cover of *Aam-Antir Bhenpu* (The mango-shell flute), a children's version of *Pather Panchali*, for which Ray had provided the cover design and all the illustrations, in an edition published by Signet Press.

RAY (*off*): . . . that the idea of turning that into a film and directing it myself occurred.

A sequence of six illustrations from *Aam-Antir Bhenpu*.

RAY (*off*): So that was that. I mean it had to be a choice of a subject and it just so happened that I knew this best and I wanted to handle children—I thought I had it in me to do so—and this business of . . .

A clipping from *Aparajito* with the camera panning over the rural countryside.

RAY (*off*): . . . the rural countryside which we knew quite well because my art director Bansi, who was then not an art director but a friend of mine . . .

Dissolve to a different landscape, the camera now panning over a countryside with hillocks in the background, until a fast-moving train passes by, the roar of the passing train blasting in on the sound-track.

RAY (*off*): . . . and me used to go on weekends into the villages. Just take a train and get off anywhere.

The *Aparajito* clip continues with the flat Bengal landscape in view again, with the familiar plants and shiny ponds reflecting the sun.

Dissolve to a close-up of Sarbajaya, looking wistfully out of the window.

Dissolve to a small rivulet flowing through high embankments, with a boy pulling a roughly made boat down the water. The camera tilts up until it catches, in silhouette, the bullock-cart passing slowly along the top of the embankment. This is what Sarbajaya sees as she looks out of the window.

Shyam Benegal, in close-up, at right of frame.

> BENEGAL: When you started making films, Mr Ray, did you feel anything . . . did you have a view about the state of cinema in India?

The camera pans completely to a close-up of Ray, now in a striped shirt, with a grilled window at his back.

> RAY: Well, we were certainly very strongly critical of the Bengali films of that period. In fact, that's one of the things that we did at the film society. We were studying foreign films—we were having seminars on things on the Indian cinema of that period. We were always strongly critical. We found most of our stuff very false, unrealistic and shoddy, commercial in a bad way. That sort of thing. They were very theatrical.

Medium shot of Ray, with Benegal, back to camera.

> BENEGAL: But when you decided to make a film, how did you go about writing a script for it?

Ray, in close-up.

> RAY: I really started as a scriptwriter with my second film when I had more confidence. What I did for my first film was . . . you see, I had to go from door to door to various distributors and producers to tell them the story in order to interest them so that they would put up the money. I did a book of drawings of the film, of frames.

A sequence of twenty sketches from his scenario for *Pather Panchali*.

BENEGAL (*off*): Yes.

RAY (*off*): Fairly elaborately done in wash, black and white, and I would tell them the story and at the same time show them the drawings, and this is what I had, even when I started the film. The actors would be given their lines a week before shooting, and we had discussions with the crew, with my assistants, with the cameraman, so we knew the set-ups more or less and we knew the trend of the story—we knew the structure of the story. For *Pather Panchali*, there was no, really no, script as such. There were notes and things like that. I had it all in my head. I mean there were notes for dialogue. Most of the dialogue came from the book. I didn't know how to write dialogue. I didn't have any confidence as a dialogue writer at that point. But fortunately Bibhutibhushan wrote very lifelike dialogue.

Ray, listening intently to Benegal, who sits with his back to the camera.

BENEGAL: One might say that there is a Satyajit Ray style of film-making, but when you look at *Pather Panchali*, for instance in the use of lenses, sometimes it appears that there is a certain arbitrariness, in the way the lenses have been used.

Ray, in close-up.

RAY: Oh, certainly, that's possible, because that's one of the hardest things to learn, which lens to use at which point. And then they didn't always have the lenses we would like to have. You know we were using three different cameras . . .

A sequence of working stills, with Ray and his crew, and his actors and actresses.

> RAY (*off*): . . . in the films. There's a Mitchell, an old Mitchell, there's an Eyemo used, and there's a Wall camera used, so whatever was available for hire, we were using, and they didn't always come with the right lenses, so that didn't leave us much of a choice. I mean we probably worked—

The camera shifts from a close-up of Ray to one of Benegal, as he starts questioning Ray. Then, as Ray answers, the camera shifts back to Ray.

> BENEGAL: But what about pacing, for instance? If you don't write a detailed script or even a treatment, how would you get an indication of how you are going to pace?
>
> RAY: Well, if you have it fairly clearly in your head, I suppose that's enough. You shoot according to what is in your head rather than what is on paper.
>
> BENEGAL (*off*): Yes.

Three shots from a book of Ray's sketches as shooting guidelines.

> RAY (*off*): Because the unit, the crew members, get to know what the story is, how the story goes, etc. But at that point since we were shooting . . .

Medium close shot of Ray, with the camera zooming slowly back.

> RAY: . . . maybe only four to five days a month, sometimes not even that, there was a six months' gap, and there was no shooting, and no money, so that was all right. There was no sort of compulsion to write a script. But we had all the time in the world to shoot the film.

Ray and Benegal in medium shot in the same position, but from a different angle now. The camera zooms to a close-up of Ray towards the end of the shot.

> RAY: In fact, we learnt filmmaking through the process of making *Pather Panchali*. We knew nothing. We were most of us new, and in fact the editor was also comparatively new. He had probably cut only one film before that, and in the final cut, at the time of final cutting, we were rushed. There's no question about that, so we might have done unorthodox things . . .

Close-up of Benegal, listening intently and nodding his head.

> RAY (*off*): . . . without realizing it.

Ray, in close-up.

> RAY: That's because the final cut was done over a period of ten days and ten nights, working all the time, because we had a deadline to catch.
>
> BENEGAL (*off*): But you did have, even if *Pather Panchali* was your first film, quite a remarkable control, particularly with the climactic moment when the husband Harihar comes back, and that was such a sophisticated thing.

A film clip from *Pather Panchali*, with Harihar coming down the path leading to the house, looking sadly at the ruins of his house, with a tree that has crashed through the wall at one side.

> RAY (*Off*): We shot the film in sequence, starting with the early part and going on chronologically, yes . . . so the early parts show a lot of rough edges, in the cutting, in the shooting, in acting, in everything, whereas I knew that all the difficult parts came in the second half . . .

Ray, in close-up.

RAY: . . . starting with the old woman's death, and then reaching a climax with Durga's death and Harihar's arrival, the father's arrival, and the very end of the film, so by that time we had learnt a little. And don't forget that it took us two years and a half to make the film, which means that we probably had some shooting one year and we had four to five months to think about it, to look at the rushes, to judge, to find out the mistakes, and not to make the same mistakes again, so it was like that . . . I feel that the second half is distinctly better made than the first half.

A film clip from *Pather Panchali*, following on the earlier sequence, the one that preceded Ray's words. Harihar enters the empty, silent courtyard, his luggage in his hands. He looks in panic at the roofless cowshed standing like a skeleton in a scene of devastation dominated by what little remains of the house with its thatched roof blown away by the storm. A cow stands in the foreground. Harihar watches it all with consternation before he calls out to the children, his voice hoarse with fear. Sarbajaya passes him by without a word, and climbs the steps to the veranda. He follows her silently.

RAY (*off*): You can see it.

The film clip continues. Harihar climbs the steps and stands on the veranda, with mixed feelings, without a clue to his wife's silence. She moves in and out of the room, bringing out a small brass pot with a long spout, pouring water into it, a low wooden seat and a towel, a pair of wooden slippers, all that her husband would need to cleanse himself with and put on before he entered the house.

HARIHAR: How are you? They've gone out, have they?

As Sarbajaya stands motionless in the foreground, Harihar takes out his gifts one by one. She holds on to her silence like a shield against the grief that is about to crush her. She barely turns her head, refusing to look at the gifts Harihar has brought home.

HARIHAR: Wouldn't I have come earlier if I could? My luck changed when I arrived at Ranaghat. It was worth all the running around I had had to do before. Here, from the chadak fair (*holding up a rolling pin and board*)—take a look. It's made of the wood of the jackfruit tree. And you'd asked me for a picture of the goddess Lakshmi, here it is. See how I have framed it in glass.

A closer shot of Harihar's hand holding an inexpensive handloom sari, which he almost forces into Sarbajaya's hand.

HARIHAR: And for Durga, there's a—here, take a look at this one. See if you like the sari. Come on, look at it. Why should you worry any more—I have come back home.

The camera tracks back slowly to bring into the frame Sarbajaya's face breaking into tears, as she clutches the sari in her hands and collapses.

She slumps down at her husband's feet, weeping bitterly, uncontrollably, shaking her head to a 'no' as Harihar's lips seem to form a question, unheard above the swelling music.

Harihar bends over her, incredulous, tries to rise in utter bewilderment, then falls back again, resting his head against Sarbajaya's shaking shoulders.

Apu, uncomprehending, stands listening to his father's sobbing—a lonely little figure, holding a big umbrella and a bottle filled with oil.

Shyam Benegal, in close-up.

> BENEGAL: Mr Ray, I am referring now to the Apu Trilogy. There's a lot that appears in that film by way of detail that is not used for information's sake but expresses much more. It expresses relationships between people, it expresses emotions at that particular time and so on. Now I can give you a few examples . . .

A film clip from *Pather Panchali*, showing the children, discovering the dead Indir Thakrun. Before the original soundtrack begins, Benegal's voice carries on with comments.

> BENEGAL (*off*): . . . say, from the little brass vessel that rolls into the water, when the old lady dies in *Pather Panchali* .

The old woman sits dead with her head sunk between her knees. Durga, without realizing this, kneels down in front of her and bends to catch her eyes, with Apu watching from behind.

Apu, watching from a distance, smiles mischievously, as if they have caught a runaway playmate.

> DURGA (*off*): Aunty!

Durga, in the same position as in the shot before the last one, is now a little scared, and shakes the old woman by the shoulder.

> DURGA: Hey, aunty!

The lifeless body rolls over, the head making a loud thud as it hits the ground.

Apu still watches in the same position as before, but now there is an uncomprehending terror in his eyes, his smile gone from his face.

Durga, in close-up, registers a look of horror as the truth dawns on her.

> DURGA (*in a whisper*): Aunty!

She stands up, scared.

In a long shot, the children run down the slope, accidentally dislodging the battered brass tumbler of the old woman, sending it tumbling down a slope into a patch of water.

The empty brass tumbler, dancing on the patch of water where it has landed, against the plaintive song that Indir once used to sing, calling her Lord to take her up to Him, now heard in the background.

The camera takes a look at the terrorized children, running away, before it tilts down slowly to focus closer on the face of the dead woman, a fly hovering on it, against the song still on the soundtrack.

Shyam Benegal, in close-up.

> BENEGAL: In *Aparajito*, there are any number of these wonderful details; for example, when Harihar is ill and he tries to button up his shirt .

Sarbajaya, her sari covering her head, comes forward, with the camera following her and bringing into view an earthen water pitcher on the floor with an inverted glass tumbler covering it, and inexpensive calendars on the wall; till she reaches her husband in bed, his face dazed with fever, his fingers fumbling with the buttons of his shirt. She moves his fingers away gently, and buttons it up for him.

BENEGAL (*off*): . . . and you know his wife comes and pushes his hands away and starts to button up . . .

A later sequence from *Aparajito*, showing Sarbajaya in a widow's garb, in medium long shot, drawing water from a well, with some broken bamboo frames at the back to support the climbing plants that bear edible fruits. There is a brass pot standing on the rim of the well.

BENEGAL (*off*): . . . and then there is the tugging of the rope, you know, at the end . . .

In a close shot, Sarbajaya turns her face at a sound, and her face breaks into a smile as she rushes out of the frame . . .

BENEGAL (*off*): . . . of the bucket on the other end of the branch, and so on.

The branch joint shaped like a Y, to which the rope is tied, registering a sudden tautening on the rope, indicating a pull.

BENEGAL (*off*): Now you haven't used very much . . .

Another sequence from *Aparajito*, showing Apu entering the house, smiling, a suitcase in one hand and a bedding in the other. He puts them down on the elevated porch in front, and as his mother rushes to him, he bends to touch her feet.

BENEGAL (*off*): . . . of that in films after that. Is there any particular reason?

Ray, in close-up.

RAY: I have been very conscious of details right from the beginning . . .

Apu, in a film clip from *Aparajito*, rushes towards the camera, circling the trunk of an ancient tree, and tumbles against a root projecting out of the ground.

> RAY (*off*): . . . and as I told you earlier, I think I mentioned it, that some of the details . . .

The film clip from *Aparajito* continues with Bhabataran, in long shot, looking obviously towards Apu, who is outside the frame. After a moment he looks away and walks off on his wooden sandals.

> RAY (*off*): . . . the idea of using details came, well, firstly from other films, from the films which I admired . . .

Apu, in close-up, stares at Bhabataran, now off frame, his apprehensions confirmed.

> RAY (*off*): . . . and also from Bibhutibhushan himself, the writer of *Pather Panchali*.

Ray, in close-up, before the crisscross grille.

> RAY: He is a writer who uses details like this often, very often, and in a very effective sort of way, which is very, very cinematic, and they can be used. For instance, there's a situation in a story which has not been filmed, where you have—I'll tell you exactly, because this is very very filmic—you have this family, the father goes insane, and it's impossible to keep him at home, and the family decides to leave him somewhere else. So the son, the young boy, and the group of elders take this mad man, just take him a couple of miles away, and leave him behind a bush, push a packet of bidis in his hand and a cigarette, and a matchbox, and just leave him there, and the boy who feels for the father suddenly turns round on the way back, and finds smoke coming out

from behind the bush. It's very very cinematic, because the mad man is smoking, you know, and that sort of thing is very cinematic, and it comes often from literature, and from Bibhutibhushan. I have used that kind of details often, so that I do not have to use words, spoken words . . .

A film clip from *Apur Sansar*, beginning with a top shot of a hackney carriage coming down a lane lined with shacks.

    RAY (*off*): . . . trying to be as expressive as possible through action, through objects, through details, things like that . . .

As the carriage pulls up, first a hand comes out to open the door by turning the handle outside, then Apu steps down and holds the door open for his new bride, who climbs out.

    APU (*to unseen coachman*): You take the luggage down. I'm coming.

Top shot of a part of a courtyard, with Apu and Aparna behind him entering through a door at one end of the courtyard, to cross from right to left of frame. The bride is still in her bridal costume, and holds the headgear of the groom in her hand.

A low angle shot of the staircase, which they climb, Aparna behind Apu, against the loud whirr of a sewing machine.

Turning a bend, Apu looks up.

A woman, back to camera, sits on the floor of a room off the staircase landing, obviously sewing at a hand machine.

Apu and Aparna climb the stairs, softly.

The elderly woman at the sewing machine, now seen from the front, with an expression of annoyance with everything in the world, half turns at the sound of footsteps, then continues with her work, with a child sitting on the floor in the foreground.

Apu and Aparna go up another flight of stairs.

Apu opens the door of the room in which he lives—a room at the top of the house, with the view beyond establishing the location of the house in one of the poorer parts of the city, with the smoke and sound of trains in the background.

From inside Apu's room, the camera watches him coming into the room, followed by Aparna.

APU: Come in. My room.

Aparna stands stiffly with the headgear of the groom in her hand, not knowing where to put it. Apu, after a little hesitation, takes it from her and moves away out of the frame. Then he comes back again.

APU: Why don't you sit down? I'll be back.

He goes away at right of the frame. Aparna hesitates for a moment. Her eyes take in the battered iron bed, like one of those in a shoddy hospital, the cheap wooden bracket on the wall with icons and a conch shell before them, and a withered garland of hibiscus flowers hanging from a peg. She moves towards the window slowly, and stands before its cheap curtain hanging.

Aparna sits down on the window sill and starts sobbing quietly. A child's laughter breaks in from some distance, with a sitar piece for effect.

Close-up of Aparna's beautiful face through the bars of the window, partly covered by the curtain. The sandalwood paste marks of the newly wed bride speak eloquently of her expectation and disappointment. Tears roll down her kohl-painted eyes, against the child's laughter bubbling in the background.

A top view of the slum adjoining their house, with a child, laughing, running towards his mother.

Aparna, watching through the bars of the window, forgets her sorrow.

Ray, in close-up.

> RAY: Sometimes you are left with no choice but to use a literary kind of symbol, as in *Jalsaghar* . . .

Biswambhar Roy, the feudal landlord, dressed in a crinkled-sleeved kurta, with a garland of white fragrant flowers around his wrist, holds a glass of wine up in his left hand, obviously offering a toast to someone.

> RAY (*off*): . . . where the problem was that this character, this zamindar . . .

The object of his toast is now held in focus by the camera—a huge oil painting of an ancestor, in the formal brocade chudidar-kurta, typical of the class, sitting regally on a chair, with one leg over the other. The camera picks out the very real spider sitting on the leg of the man in the portrait.

> RAY (*off*): . . . was the only one on the screen for minutes on end, there was no communication, no verbal communication with anybody.

Horrified, Biswambhar Roy brings down his hand with the glass, and the smile vanishes from his lips. He raises the walking stick held in his right hand and walks towards the portrait.

> RAY (*off*): One could perhaps have used words on the soundtrack, but that again would have been even more literary, conveying his thoughts in a stream of consciousness kind of thing.

The portrait of the ancestor in long shot, with Biswambhar Roy, back to camera, proceeding towards it with his stick raised.

> RAY (*off*): But then one has to use it when you are left with no other choice but to use that kind of a literary . . .

In a close shot, the spider scampers away, chased by the end of the walking stick. The camera moves upwards to hold the smiling face of the portrait in frame.

> RAY (*off*): . . . which I'm not very fond of myself frankly.

Biswambhar Roy, in the scene from *Jalsaghar*, now triumphant, walks back, laughing at his own victory and the plight of the spider.

> RAY (*off*): But at other times, I think, even after the Trilogy . . .

Ray, in close-up.

> RAY: . . . even in films like *Charulata* and others you find details of this nature.

Benegal, in close-up.

> BENEGAL: But when you are already at the script stage, now with Bibhutibhushan's novels, you've of course mentioned this, but when you're yourself working them out, does it happen at that scripting stage, or when you are actually starting to shoot . . .

Ray, in close-up.

> BENEGAL (*off*): . . . that it might occur to you . . . ?

> RAY: Well, very important details can be there at the script stage itself. But details of action as you suggest, for example, that in *Aparajito*, where you have the father trying to button up his shirt, but being ill, the wife, you know, sort of does it for him, you know . . . that sort of thing probably often happens at the stage of filming, at the time of filming. You suddenly have an idea which will make a shot or a scene or an action more expressive, more telling, that you always . . . there is always room for improvisation of that nature . . .

Benegal, in close-up, listening intently.

> RAY (*off*): . . . during shooting.

Ray, in close-up, till camera shifts to a close-up of Benegal in profile.

> BENEGAL: The Trilogy shows yet another quality which I don't believe was part of the Indian cinema at all until that time, which is that you don't use what one might call the automatically information scenes, scenes that are obligatory, that explain particular situations and so on. There are, I mean, very, very few scenes in the Trilogy where you might say that this is an information scene. You have been able . . .

A film clip from *Apur Sansar* begins with Apu and Pulu, at left and right of frame respectively, walking towards the camera, deep in conversation, along a dimly lit Calcutta street at night. Benegal's voice, heard over the soundtrack, gives way to Apu's voice on the original soundtrack.

> BENEGAL (*off*): . . . like in *Apur Sansar*, for instance, when your Apu is talking about his novel, you know, on the tracks, and when he starts to talk about the book he is going to

write, which is really his autobiography, this is done with such economy .

APU: A young boy . . .

PULU: Huh?

APU: A . . . young boy . . .

PULU: All right.

APU: A village boy.

PULU: Very well.

Apu's face, in close-up, animated, as he speaks of his dream novel.

APU: Poor, but sensitive. (*Smiles*). The father is a priest, and he dies.

PULU: Hmm.

APU (*dreamily*): The boy comes to the city. He will not be a priest, he will study. He is ambitious. Through his education, his struggle, we see him shedding his old superstitions, his orthodoxy. He must use his intellect. He cannot accept anything blindly. But he has imagination. He is sensitive. Little things move him, give him joy. He may have in him the seeds of greatness, but . . .

PULU: He doesn't make it.

APU (*enthusiastic*): . . . he doesn't. But that is not the last word. It is not a tragedy. He does nothing great. He remains poor, in want. But in spite of that, he never turns away from life. He doesn't run away, he doesn't escape. He wants to live. He says that the act of living is in itself a fulfilment, in it lies happiness. (*Excited.*) He wants to live.

PULU (*off*): No.

APU (*deflated*): What do you mean?

The camera tracks back slowly, leaving the two friends facing each other, fiercely waving their arms in the heat of the arguing.

PULU: Where's the novel? It's your own story!

APU (*defiant*): Some of it is autobiographical. A lot of it is fiction. Besides, there are imaginary characters, there's a plot, the love interest.

PULU: What? Love?

APU: Why not?

PULU (*astounded*): Love?

APU (*insistent*): Why not?

PULU: What do you know of love?

APU: Why?

PULU: What can you know about love? Have you ever been within ten yards of a girl? Have you any experience of love?

APU (*shouting*): Does one have to experience everything?

PULU (*shouting back*): Certainly. You can't cheat!

APU: Is imagination worth nothing?

PULU: Nothing. Where love is concerned. Not a thing.

APU: Who told you?

PULU: I am telling you.

APU: Rubbish! You know nothing. If a man has talent . . .

PULU: Yes?

APU: He can do anything.

PULU: No!

Benegal, in close-up, from the side, with the camera moving to hold Ray in close-up by the time the shot closes.

BENEGAL: But in the later films sometimes you find those obligatory scenes, you know. There is direct information.

RAY: I think they arise out of the material, which you cannot help sometimes. Sometimes you have to use a conventional method, sometimes you can do without them. I don't think that the methods which I used in *Apur Sansar* and the other Trilogy films I do not find useful any more, or it's just because of that, that I've stopped using them. It's just that I've been using different kinds, other kinds of material which demand other kinds of treatment.

Medium close shot of Ray, his hand against his chin, listening to Benegal out of the frame, and then lifting his head to look in the direction of Benegal as he answers.

BENEGAL (*off*): Was there a kind of autobiographical resonance in this film?

RAY: Well, not in *Pather Panchali* frankly, because I know hardly anything about village life. I was a city-born and city-bred person, and I didn't know the village at all till the age of thirty—twenty-five or thirty—but in the second part the fact of Apu's adolescence and his mother being a widow—the mother and son relationship—that can have autobiographical elements in it certainly, because I was in a similar situation.

BENEGAL (Off): Did you identify with Apu?

RAY: I suppose one does. One has to, particularly when you deal with a character through three films right from his childhood to adulthood. You do identify, otherwise there is no getting under the skin of the character.

BENEGAL (*off*): But tell me, did you plan it as a trilogy when you first started *Pather Panchali*?

RAY (*shaking his head*): Oh, no, no, no, no question of that. In fact, I couldn't see beyond just that one film at that point when I made *Pather Panchali*. It was only after the acceptance of *Pather Panchali* by the public in Calcutta itself, before it won prizes or anything, that I really decided to give up advertising and go into filmmaking. When I looked for a second subject for a while, then it suddenly struck me, why not make another film about Apu? Well, there was this other book *Aparajito* left. I made it, and then, even then, even after making *Aparajito* I didn't have a trilogy in mind, because *Aparajito* was a failure at the box office. Since it was a failure I had to think of doing something completely different. I did a comedy that worked reasonably well, and then I did *Jalsaghar—The Music Room*; because even *Parashpathar*, the comedy, wasn't such a success. So I was again in doubt about what kind of a film to make, and I decided to make a film about music and dancing, the conventional, the sort of formula that the Bengali public was used to, although in developing it, it became a completely different kind of film. It was not a light-hearted commercial sort of thing at all.

A film clip from *Jalsaghar*, with two feet in close-up, with dancing bells around the ankles, moving in rhythm to the beat of the tabla.

Sharp cut to two hands moving fast in close-up on the surface of the pair of percussion instruments.

Biswambhar Roy, enjoying the dance, half reclining on a pillow.

The dancing feet again in close-up.

The dancing girl goes through her routine of spectacular whirls, in the grand music room, with the ornate table at one corner, the bronze candlestands shaped like statues.

A long shot brings the whole room into view, with the spectators, including the host, Biswambhar Roy, sitting, back to camera, as the dancing girl bows to her august audience at the end of her performance. As she bows, there is a roar of appreciation from the spectators. The grand setting includes a huge mirror against the far wall, a multi-tiered chandelier hanging from the ceiling, and the accompanists sitting with their sarangi and the pair of percussion instruments.

Mahim Sarkar, the rich upstart who seems to challenge the traditional authority of the landlord, Biswambhar Roy, is part of the audience. He throws up his hands in appreciation, and then brings a fistful of coins out of his pocket, to offer them as a reward to the dancing girl.

    MAHIM: Long live the Baiji! It was great.

In a dramatic close-up, the curved head of Biswambhar Roy's walking stick restrains Mahim's hand.

Mahim's face in close-up, looking back at Biswambhar Roy, registering at once how deeply he has been offended.

Ray, in close-up.

    RAY: After *Aparajito* had won the prize at Venice, at the Press Conference I was asked whether I had a trilogy in mind, and I found myself saying, Yes.

A sequence of designs for posters and hoardings, all designed by Ray, for *Apur Sansar* and *Jalsaghar*.

BENEGAL (*off*): Mr Ray, in your work there seems to be certain distinct changes that have occurred particularly after *Charulata*. In the beginning, in most of the films that you handled there was a very distinct lyrical kind of approach that appeared to be missing in a couple of films in between which seem like aberrations, but it concludes with *Charulata*, and then you have a different kind of sensibility starting to operate. What do you think is the reason for this?

Ray, in close-up.

RAY: One thing which I have tried to do is not to repeat myself thematically. I made the Trilogy, OK; but in between I had made a comedy, and I had made a film about the past, about a zamindar, and then again I have gone back to that from time to time.

Close-up of a poster for *Devi*, with the camera slowly moving over it from bottom to top.

RAY (*off*): *Devi* was about the nineteenth century.

A film clip from *Devi* with Kalikinkar (played by Chhabi Biswas, seen already as Biswambhar Roy in *Jalsaghar*), approaching his daughter-in-law, who stands with bowed head, covered with the edge of her sari, in front of her father-in-law.

KALIKINKAR: Mother!

Kalikinkar's elder son rushes out of his bedroom, wrapping a shawl around himself hurriedly.

Kalikinkar, staring at his daughter-in-law, lowers himself at her feet.

KALIKINKAR: Mother, why didn't you tell us before?

As his head touches the ground at her feet, Dayamayee's toes curl in natural reaction.

Taraprasad, the elder son, rushes to his father, in shock and disbelief.

He reaches his father, and bends down to raise him.

 TARAPRASAD: Father, what are you doing?

As the camera holds Kalikinkar in close-up, he looks up slowly at his son.

 KALIKINKAR: Kneel to her, Tara, and touch her feet. In my dreams
  I was told that she is the goddess incarnate.

Dayamayee turns her head to the wall, trying to hide behind the sari that covers her head. Her helpless fingers clutch at the wall.

 KALIKINKAR (*off*): All my prayers have borne fruit today.

The enraptured father and the incredulous son in medium close shot, with Kalikinkar kneeling down again and going out of frame.

 KALIKINKAR: My life finds meaning at last.

Taraprasad's wife (played by Karuna Banerjee, Sarbajaya in the Apu Trilogy), listening from her bedroom door, backs away in shocked disbelief.

Ray, in close-up.

 RAY: I think a director is fascinated not only by theme or subject
  matter, but also by certain visual aspects of a story. I'm
  interested in recreating the past in the visual aspect of opulence, for instance. That fascinates me very much. So I occasionally do that. And *Charulata* was certainly a culmination
  of that.

In a clip from *Charulata*, Charulata comes out of her bedroom and turns right, with the camera following her along the long covered corridor until she crosses a door.

The camera now looks at another part of the same corridor, in long shot, at right angle to the first, with Charu coming over a mosaic floor, passing semicircular marble-top tables along the wall with bronze sculptures upon them. The doors to the rooms on the left have etched-glass panes, completing the picture of opulence. Charu enters one of the doors.

The library that Charu enters at the far end from right underlines the same opulence with its papered walls, the chandelier, upholstered chairs with ornately carved arms and legs, and corner and wall cabinets with elaborate carvings. Charu comes closer to the camera, and opens a bookcase.

Her heavily bangled hand, in close-up, replaces a book. In a medium shot, she looks over the other books, trying to choose a book to read. She hums, 'Bankim, Bankim . . ', the name of an author she has in mind, and whose book—*Kapalakundala*—she eventually finds.

Her attention is suddenly diverted by the fast rat-tat of the small drum a monkey-player in the street below uses to draw the crowd. She turns her back to camera, still humming to herself, and walks unhurriedly down the long room, looking into the book in her hand, till she reaches a window, and opens the blind to look out, obviously at the monkey and the player.

A view of the monkey-player down below, standing in the compound of a neighbour's house, from behind the window blind, as he still rattles his drum to attract spectators.

Close-up of Charu's absorbed profile, till she suddenly thinks of something.

She moves at a fast pace, obviously with a purpose, out of the library, across the long corridor, towards her bedroom, the camera following her.

From behind the ornate headboard of her bed, the camera watches Charu entering her bedroom. She walks down fast, to a sideboard, pulls out a drawer and takes out a pair of opera glasses, as the camera comes closer to her on a trolley around the bed. The drum of the monkey player keeps rattling on the soundtrack.

Charu's hand swinging the pair of glasses moves on, in close-up, the camera moving with it.

Charu looks out of the open blind, this time through the opera glasses.

A closer view of the monkey player, even as he walks out of the range of her lens.

Charu's face in close-up, disappointment writ large on it. She puts down the glasses for a moment, but a strange sound—the rhythmic call of the palanquin bearers—breaks upon the scene, and draws her to another window where again she opens the blinds and looks out, putting the glasses to her eyes. It has now become a game for her to kill time.

The palanquin bearers move from left to right, as Charu's opera glasses pick them up. A fat man with a well-oiled head and an umbrella held over it passes from right to left in the space on which the glasses focus.

Charu's head moves slightly as she follows the fat man with a smile on her lips.

The monkey player's drum rattles faintly, but by now Charu's interest has shifted to the ridiculous fat man. She comes out of the library and moves across the drawing room to open yet another window.

The fat man comes into view again, moving from right to left, as Charu watches him.

Charu shuts the blind and moves to the next window, to follow the man a little further.

Again the fat man passes from right to left of frame.

This window is also shut, as Charu shifts to another window.

Now she can hear the sing-song call of a hawker peddling utensils. Charu watches the pedlar passing by, with a boy behind him, and then the fat man again, till he finally goes out of her range of vision, not to be seen any more.

A long shot of the big hall, with Charu standing alone at the far end, lonely amidst all this opulence, time hanging heavy on her hands. She moves through the room in leisurely pace, lightly touching all the objects one by one, until she reaches the piano. She sits on the stool before it and opens the lid of the piano, clearly in want of anything better to do. She suddenly hears footsteps, and looks up expectantly.

Ray, in close-up.

RAY: But after that I decided, perhaps it's difficult to recall the state of mind that prompts you to do certain things, I perhaps felt, maybe I came across certain contemporary stories by young writers which dealt with the contemporary local problems of Calcutta at that time, and I decided to, again for a change, to do some of those stories.

BENEGAL (*off*): Would you say that you knew that the environment was changing around you, and there was the effect of that on you?

RAY: Well, that . . . that did happen towards the end of the sixties, the early seventies. I could describe that as a period in which you strongly felt certain changes taking place, almost in the day to day existence, you felt it, and you felt that without that you couldn't make a film.

A film clip from *Pratidwandi* (*The Adversary*) begins, with two elderly men, in formal clothes, interviewing Siddhartha, the protagonist, for a job.

MEMBER OF THE PANEL: Who was the prime minister of England at the time of Independence?

Siddhartha, in medium shot, at the other side of the table.

SIDDHARTHA: Whose Independence, sir?

The Member of the Panel, in close-up.

MEMBER OF THE PANEL: Our Independence.

Siddhartha, in close-up.

SIDDHARTHA: Attlee.

The other Member of the Panel, in close-up, his turn now to ask.

MEMBER OF THE PANEL: What do you regard as the most outstanding and significant event of the last decade?

Close-up of Siddhartha, thinking.

The Members of the Panel, facing Siddhartha, back to camera.

Siddhartha, still thinking.

Close-up of one Member of the Panel.

Close-up of the other Member of the Panel.

Siddhartha arrives at an answer.

SIDDHARTHA: The War in Vietnam, sir.

The Members of the Panel, with inscrutable faces.

MEMBER OF THE PANEL: More significant than the landing on the moon?

SIDDHARTHA (*off*): I think so, sir.

Close-up of Siddhartha, waiting for their response.

The Members of the Panel, on the other side of the table.

MEMBER OF THE PANEL: Could you tell us why you think so?

The camera goes behind the Members of the Panel, to catch Siddhartha in a top shot, as he tries to explain his feelings and convictions with deadly honesty.

SIDDHARTHA: Because the moon landing—you see . . . we . . . we weren't entirely unprepared for the moon landing. We knew it had to come some time. We knew about the space flights, the great advances in space technology. So we knew it had to happen. I am not saying it wasn't a remarkable achievement, but it wasn't unpredictable, the fact that they did land on the moon.

The camera focuses on the Members of the Panel across the table, with Siddhartha, back to camera at left of the frame.

MEMBER OF THE PANEL: Do you think that the War in Vietnam was unpredictable?

Siddhartha, in close-up.

SIDDHARTHA: Not the war itself, but what it has revealed about the Vietnamese people, about their extraordinary power of resistance. Ordinary people, peasants . . . no one knew they had it in them. It isn't a matter of technology . . . it's . . . it's just plain human courage, and it . . . it takes your breath away.

The Members of the Panel, in close-up, nod gravely, with one of them sitting back, clearly unsure about this unexpected reply.

Close-up of Siddhartha, waiting.

One of the Members has made up his mind.

MEMBER OF THE PANEL: Are you a Communist?

Siddhartha, in close-up.

SIDDHARTHA: I don't think one has to *be* a Communist in order to admire Vietnam, sir.

MEMBER OF THE PANEL: That doesn't answer my question.

Close-up of Siddhartha, watching, waiting for their verdict. The voice is carried over from the last shot to bring the film clip to a close.

MEMBER OF THE PANEL: However . . .

Benegal, in close-up.

BENEGAL: You set a certain kind of photographic style when you made your first film, because Indian films used to rely a great deal on what one might call a manufactured kind of feel and look, which was highly cosmetic, and did a great deal for the main actors, you know, to make them look good, and so on, and you changed it. Was there a very conscious attempt on your part?

Ray, in close-up.

RAY: It was very, very conscious. It was something I discussed with my cameraman right at the start of the shooting. We were both great admirers of Cartier-Bresson.

A black and white composition by Cartier-Bresson. The natural source of light at right is not disturbed by any light from the left, so that the contrast of black and white on the bodies and faces of the characters stands out sharply. In fact, the natural light brings out clearly even the grains on the wall.

RAY (*off*): And we believed in available light, the source of the light, for photography, I mean maintaining the sources as far as possible . . .

The same Cartier-Bresson photograph, now from a longer distance, emphasizing its authenticity.

RAY (*off*): . . . and for the day scenes, unless there was sunlight.

Ray, in close-up.

RAY: Well, for location, you chose certain times of the day to shoot certain scenes. In fact, before we started we discussed this with a lot of film people, and they said, you can't shoot in the rain, you can't shoot on a dull day, you can't do this, you, can't do that. So we made some experiments with 16 mm camera shooting, and all kinds of light conditions, and we found that everything came out. So we decided to do the realistic kind of photography.

An outdoor shot in broad daylight, from *Pather Panchali*, with Apu, now a boy of ten, chewing a piece of sugarcane, with a tinsel crown on his head.

APU: Didi, what are those?

Close-up of Durga in profile, as she looks up and pouts her lips, indicating that she does not know, nor cares.

APU (*off*): If mother only . . .

Durga hears something in the distance, and stops Apu abruptly, to listen more carefully. Then her lips form the word: 'Train?'

The two children stand up in excitement and look around for the source of the sound, till they detect the wisp of smoke puffing out in the distance, and start running towards it.

The children, in long shot, run through the billowing fields of the white kaash flowers. The dense smoke from the engine blackens the sky as the train chugs on, passing from right to left of the frame.

Long shot of the train, small in the distant horizon, with the camera panning to the running children.

The children, in long shot, run towards the camera through the kaash fields.

The train passes close in front of the camera, with the fields beyond seen in glimpses between the running wheels. When the train is gone, Apu can be seen, standing, small and insignificant, in the field, all by himself.

A long shot of the darkening sky above the kaash fields, the rain clouds hanging heavy.

Ray, in close-up.

> RAY: But really the available light problem showed up when we were shooting in the studio, because for the day scenes, for instance, the normal practice in those days was to use direct lights which would cast shadows all around, and I hated the idea of having characters move across a wall or something casting shadows, and the shadows moving at the same time. So we started using bounce lights, not so much in *Pather Panchali*, because in *Pather Panchali* the only day scenes were night scenes—only the studio scenes were night scenes—and that didn't involve available light or bounce lighting to that extent. But in *Aparajito* for instance, in the house which was built in the studio, the house in which the family lived, and the only source of light there as in the

usual Banaras houses was from above the courtyard, which was open and from where you could see the sky if you looked up, and we had a cloth stretched right across the top and the lights were bounced off the cloth there to suggest a kind of top source . . .

An excerpt from *Aparajito* shows the courtyard of a shabby house, with an entrance from the road at the far end, and at close left, a water tank with a top. Sarbajaya is seen cleaning the courtyard with a broomstick and a pail of water. Harihar enters by the door, obviously after a bath in the holy Ganga. He has a bundle of wet clothes in his hand, which he hangs to dry on the clothes line, before going out at right of the frame.

> RAY (*off*): . . . a top indirect source, not the sunlight, but when using the sunlight as a source through a window or somewhere, we were using direct lights all the time.

Benegal, in close-up.

> BENEGAL: When you started making films you used to rely entirely on block lenses, and once the zoom came in, you never left the zoom. Any particular reason . . . ?

Ray, listening, at the beginning of the shot, with Benegal, back to camera, till camera zooms slowly to hold Ray in a close-up, leaving Benegal out of frame.

> BENEGAL: . . . in that change of style?
>
> RAY: I think we used the zoom for the first time in *Charulata*, and that was the time when I started operating the camera also. Formerly my cameraman would operate, but then I started using, operating myself, because I felt that looking through the Arriflex, that was the best position to watch

the action from, and with the zoom—not that I used to zoom a great deal—but with the zoom—I think we were using the blimp zoom—I found it was very convenient in long dialogue scenes to zoom occasionally very slightly for emphasis—which was not rehearsed, but improvised, let us say. While watching through the lens I felt at certain points that if I got a little closer or a little further away it would help, and this was almost like using the zoom as a substitute for tracking. But a very, very slight zoom. At other points I occasionally used the zoom as a sort of flourish. It's hard to sort of describe it without examples, but there is for instance a shot in *Charulata* which comes at the end of the first long sequence of Charu being alone, and establishing her loneliness, and the very last shot is where she watches her husband through the opera glasses, and then she, well, obviously arrives at some sort of conclusion, and the opera glasses come down like that, and there we zoom back immediately to a mid-shot from a close-up, and that ends this sequence. It is sort of a flourish as you put a flourish at the end of an article or a letter.

An excerpt from *Charulata*, with Charu, back to camera, at right of frame, watching her husband Bhupati going down a long corridor, with his back to camera and Charu.

Charu, in close-up, puts the opera glasses to her eyes and looks at her husband through them.

Bhupati, her husband, already at the other end of the long corridor, turns right towards the staircase and goes down, out of Charu's sight.

Charu, in close-up, slowly takes the glasses off her eyes, and then her hand with the glasses swings downwards. Simultaneously, the camera zooms back from Charu, giving a flourish to the end. The image that comes through ultimately is one of a woman, young, beautiful and lonely.

Ray, in close-up.

> RAY: Then again, I felt, if I wanted to get very close to a character right up here, normally it would mean tracking on a dolly, bringing the camera right up to here, but it would be disturbing for the actors, and then with a zoom you could have the camera at a distance and then zoom in to a very big close-up.

Another excerpt from *Charulata*, with the camera touching several treetops, crossing a boundary wall between the houses, before it stops at a neighbour's first floor veranda, following Charu's viewpoint, to focus on a mother there playing with a child.

> RAY (*off*): This happened again in *Charulata* when Charu is on the swing and has her memories of her childhood . . .

In a close-up, Charu's hand holds the opera glasses to her eyes, with the camera zooming slowly to very close to her face, picking up a tiny frown that mars the serenity of her expression.

> RAY (*off*): . . . and gradually, gradually very slowly I bring the zoom forward which couldn't be done with a dolly.

Benegal, in close-up.

> BENEGAL: We are aware of course that with the block lens the character and the environment have a certain kind of relationship which does not arbitrarily change. Once you use a

zoom this tends to change because the perspective tends to get flashy.

Ray, in close-up, till the camera trolleys back to hold him in medium shot.

> RAY: Yes, it does actually. I would never or very seldom use a zoom as a substitute for a trolley. But for certain things, for instance, a man suddenly notices an object, which has a certain importance for him, and he reacts to it—and then we show the object—formerly we would dolly in if we wanted a certain emphasis.

A film clip from *Charulata*, with Charu, in close-up, looking down at something, deep in thought, her two hands covering her mouth.

> RAY (*off*): But obviously the character is not walking towards the object . . .

A pair of men's slippers lie on the carpet, with the camera zooming slowly towards it.

> RAY (*off*): . . . but the object is being brought forward.

Charu, in close-up, registering the dawning of a thought.

> RAY (*off*): So I thought the zoom would be more logical to use in those circumstances.

Benegal, in close-up.

> BENEGAL: I remember once reading somewhere about the way you locate. You know, say, you go shooting on a location, and when you build a set, there are some very distinct positions where you are likely to shoot from. That's how the set is designed. But when it comes to going on a location, there

is, you have always said that, you know you cannot leave the familiar. There are two or three familiar positions that you are likely to take, and that's how the place gets located and recognized. I would like really for you to add something on that because I myself have learnt a great deal from it.

Ray, in close-up.

RAY: Well, I don't think that I was particularly aware of that when I made my first film. For instance, in *Pather Panchali*, we had this house with the courtyard, the old woman's house, the main part of the house, and the kitchen, and perhaps I should have stuck to certain specific positions in order for the geography to be clearer to the audience. But watching *Pather Panchali* today, I find that I haven't done that to that extent. So perhaps the audience takes a little longer to realize in which part or where the old woman's house is situated, where the kitchen is situated. But on location I think you don't have to be, you can't afford to be so specific in your angles, because you change your angles. Sometimes the light dictates a change. Sometimes you discover new interesting angles which you didn't discover when for the first time you found the location. That happens during the shooting all the time, but with this in mind, you mustn't confuse the geography very much.

Benegal, in close-up.

BENEGAL: Now before you came on the scene in the Indian cinema, certainly there never used to be what one might call an ambient sound, an effect outside of the synchronized effects. You started it. Now why did you do it? What led you to use sound like that?

Ray, in close-up.

RAY: I think in the use of sound, we were not being very original. We were doing what the best European cinema had done, which we admired very much. We didn't really learn from the Indian cinema. We learnt in fact what not to do rather than what to do. So we had the examples of the best cinema of the West, that is what we had in mind. With *Pather Panchali* as well as *Aparajito*, there was this question of filling long stretches of silence because both films had very little dialogue. Naturally we had to think of what to do there and all sorts of sound effects and music were used in order basically to fill those long stretches of silence and also at the same time for them to work as ambient sound.

BENEGAL (*off*): But didn't you suddenly come upon . . .

Benegal, in close-up.

BENEGAL: . . . the idea that this could also be used creatively, because obviously . . . but after that . . .

Ray, in close-up.

RAY: Yes, yes, but both things came at the same time. I think you have to have both in mind, creatively, in the sense that you add to the atmosphere, you also suggest things which are not suggested by the dialogue or by the images. So that's another dimension to the film.

An excerpt from *Pratidwandi*, with Siddhartha's sister in medium shot, turning her head to admonish.

SISTER: Dada!

Siddhartha, in close-up, looks up, in silence.

The camera zooms to a close-up of Siddhartha's sister.

A LITTLE GIRL'S VOICE (*off*): Hey, Dada!

The camera takes a low angle view of a little girl, the sister, when younger, with a bright face, obviously a flashback.

GIRL: Listen to that strange bird calling.

Long shot of a little boy sitting on the ground, against an undulating landscape and trees all around.

BOY: Where?

Low angle shot of the little girl putting her finger to her lips. A long shot of the sister, listening intently.

SISTER: Sh-h-h-

The bird's whistle sounds distinctly on a landscape in long shot, of treetops with the sun shining through them.

A long shot of the sister, listening intently.

SISTER: There it is!

The boy rises to his feet, in long shot.

BROTHER: Great!

The little boy, in medium shot, listening intently, and smiling in delight, looks to the right of the frame, and asks someone out of frame.

BROTHER: Bhajua, what's this bird called?

From the flashback, we return to the present, with Siddhartha, sitting in brooding silence, seen through the bars of a window. He tries to light a cigarette, but the old birdcall is heard on the soundtrack, and he looks up at once to face the camera, which slowly zooms to him.

The camera, obviously placed outside the door, catches Siddhartha standing up slowly and walking out of the door. He crosses the terrace, with the camera following him, till he comes to stand near the balustrade. With his back to the camera, he looks at the distant fields, across which a procession of corpse bearers comes up, their chant *Ramnam Sat Hai* (Rama's name is the only truth)—heard indistinctly. Siddhartha slowly turns towards the camera, as the shot freezes.

Benegal, in close-up.

> BENEGAL: You have also done a great deal in the use of music, because when you started there would be a thematic score, and there also used to be a lot of incidental music, which over a period of time you have not used. I mean, incidental music, particularly to underline, say, an emotional moment or a climactic moment—things like that. How have you . . . have you thought of the way you have evolved in the use of music itself?

Ray, in close-up, against grilled window.

> RAY: Well, in the beginning, of course, I was not my own composer. I was using other composers like Ravi Shankar and Vilayat Khan and Ali Akbar. I worked with them . . . but I always knew where the music would come, and this was . . . I had to tell the composers beforehand that these are the points where I needed music. And so that was done. And this, of course, led to some difficulties because I was

getting musical ideas of my own at that time, and it was difficult to dictate to professionals . . . I mean, they were not professional film composers, they were virtuosos really. Ravi Shankar particularly was very gifted also in this direction because he had done ballet scores and all that. And that's how we worked and later, of course, I took over composing myself.

Ray's working room, in a long shot, with the camera panning slowly across a shelf and a table full of books, till it comes to hold Ray at the piano, composing.

> RAY (*off*): Because, for one thing most of the time they were not available, and for another I felt that since I couldn't think of other composers to use. I didn't think there were very many good professional film composers, I started doing it myself. Well, I have a piano, which I strum, but I also hum and whistle a great deal.

Close-up of a row of figurines won as awards by Ray, decorating the piano top, with the camera panning to Ray, playing the piano.

> RAY (*off*): But over the years of course I have come to the point where I use less and less music. Music is something which I always feel is, after a point, a dispensable element. One uses music more with the public in mind than anything else, because one is afraid that the public will not be able to get . . . the mood of a certain scene . . .

Ray, in profile, playing at the piano.

> RAY (*off*): . . . and you want to underline it so that they don't miss it. It is unfortunate, but you have to do it. I'm trying to be economical with music.

The camera holds Ray in the same position for a while, but this time from a little further off, before it starts panning around the room revealing shelves laden with books.

> RAY (*off*): Oh, there are other reasons for that too. We have lost most of our musicians. They have gone to Bombay now.

Ray, in close up.

> RAY: So we have to be content with second-rate players mostly. So one has to be inventive and use simpler things.

Benegal, in close-up.

> BENEGAL: For instance, the Trilogy has one of the most beautiful thematic lines.

Ray, in close-up.

> RAY: Oh, that! I have always believed in having leitmotifs which would reappear in a film from time to time to give it a sort of unity. For instance, the main theme of *Pather Panchali* was a brilliant invention of Ravi Shankar's. He had the theme in mind even before he saw the film.

In a film clip from *Pather Panchali*, Durga and Apu go down the village path, in a long shot, with their backs to the camera which watches them steadily. A stout man crosses them, turns to look at them for once, and continues walking towards the camera, till he goes out of the frame, and the children become smaller in the dis tance. Throughout the shot there is a soft folk motif playing on a flute, backed by the sitar.

Ray, in close-up.

> BENEGAL (*off*): Your musical ideas are Indian, or Western, or . . .

RAY: No, it depends on the film really, because for a film like *Pather Panchali*, or perhaps any of the Trilogy films, it would have to be Indian to a large extent, but I have also tried fusions—fusions between Indian and Western idioms. This I do constantly in films that deal with contemporary Calcutta, for instance, which in itself is a kind of fusion . . . the life style . . .

A film clip from *Mahanagar*, with the camera following the overhead line of the tramway track, with the polehead of a tram car running along it, and the credit titles superimposed. On the soundtrack, a fully orchestrated piece of music with tablas, trumpets, flutes, etc. grows faster, building up to a climax as the shot ends with the title:

SCRIPT, MUSIC, DIRECTION
SATYAJIT RAY

Ray, in close-up.

RAY: I have been interested in music since my schooldays—in Western classical music to start with, and then also I got interested in Indian classical music as well, and I developed the habit of listening to Western classical music with a miniature score and that used to be my bedside reading. I would listen to a piece, a new symphony perhaps, with a score, and then go to bed with it, and going through it, the symphony would come back to me, and that's how I learnt . . .

Three pages of Western notation of musical pieces, in Ray's own handwriting, in three consecutive shots.

RAY (*off*): . . . Western notation. I mean I didn't learn consciously at that time, but when I decided to compose, I had to teach myself the Western notation, but later I discovered that most of the musicians here know the Bengali notation . . .

FIGURE 32. Satyajit Ray as a child.

FIGURES 33–41. (*Above and facing page*) Oddities and grotesques: illustrations by Sukumar Ray, who 'had an absolutely unique style of doing comic illustrations'.

FIGURE 42. Ray as commercial artist: an advertisement for Paludrine, 'very very filmic'.

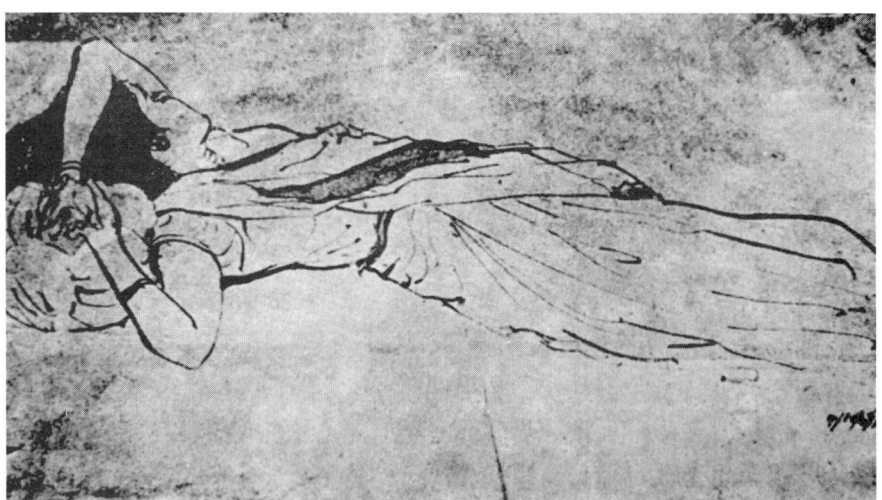

FIGURE 43. A drawing of a sleeping woman.

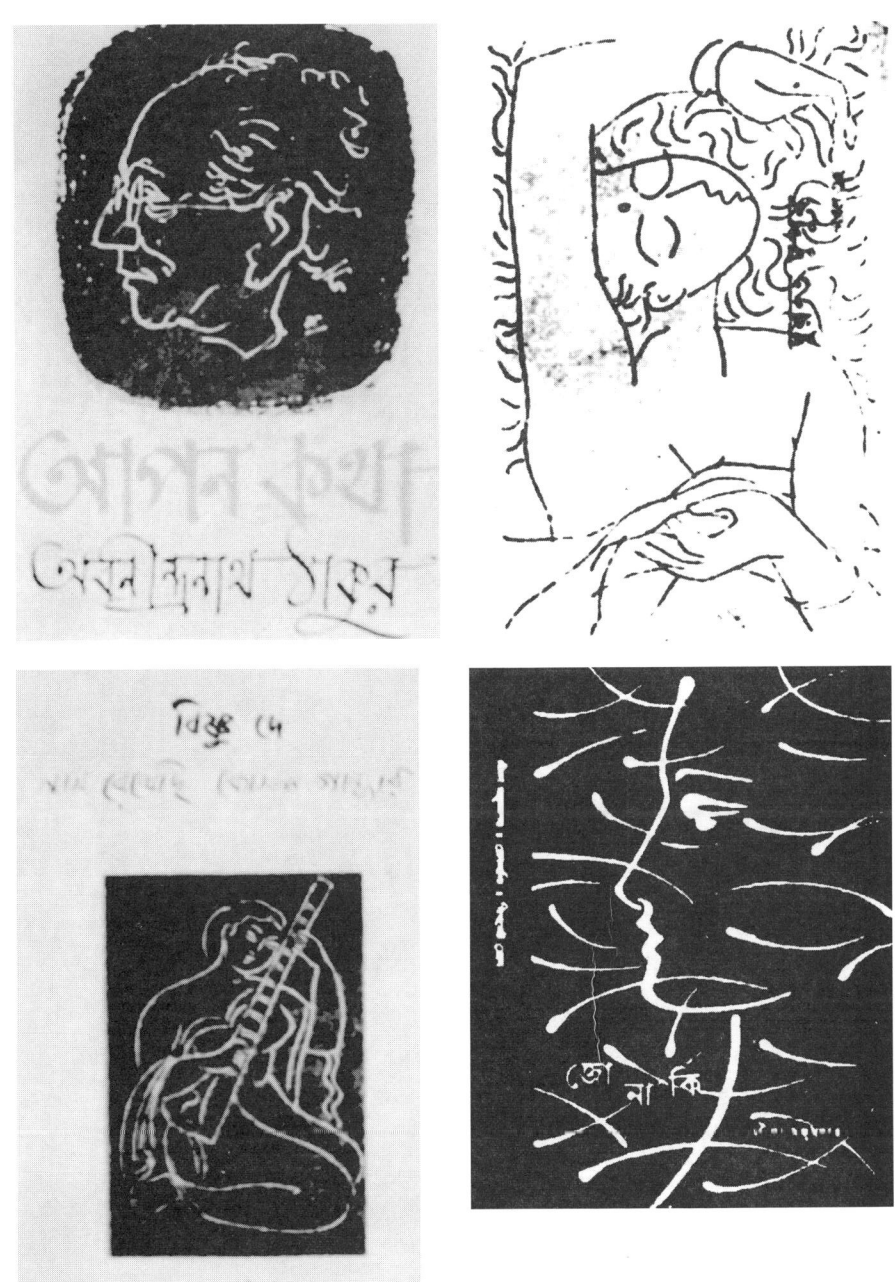

FIGURES 44–47. Book covers for Signet Press, designed by Ray.

FIGURES 48–51. Portraits and caricatures by Ray: Eisenstein and Picasso (*top*), and Dilip Kumar and Nargis (*bottom*): 'in my early school days my main interest was stars . . . early in college . . . I became aware of the director.'

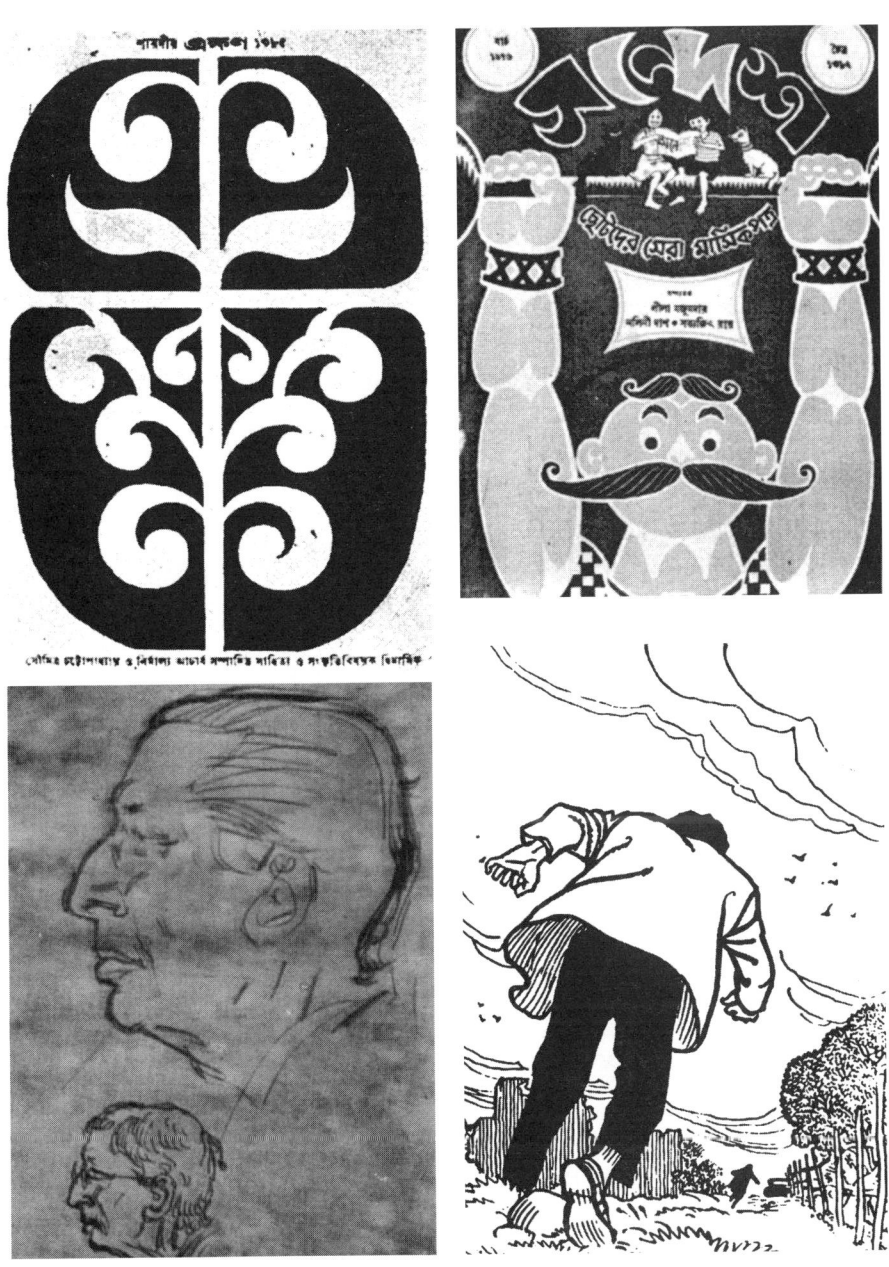

FIGURES 52-55. Covers for periodicals (*top*): *Ekshan* for the intellectuals, *Sandesh* for children; the way he envisaged Kanu Bandyopadhyay for a role in a film never made (*bottom left*); and a sketch for one of his own stories (*bottom right*).

FIGURES 56–58. An illustration by Ray for a story by Leela Majumdar in *Sandesh* (*top*); a title page illustration for a book of poems by Naresh Guha (*bottom left*), and a sketch for a poster for *Tin Kanya* (*bottom right*).

A page of handwritten notation, this time written in Bengali.

> RAY (*off*): . . . only. But when there's a violinist who knows the Western notation, it is converted on the spot and given to him.

Ray, in close-up.

> RAY: Of course, I am a composer only fifteen days of the year. The rest of the time, nothing—the piano is shut, it is not used at all. It gathers dust, that sort of thing.

Benegal, in close-up.

> BENEGAL: As far as editing is concerned, do you keep to a fairly conventional scheme in the style of editing in your films? Haven't you felt the need, for instance, to break out of that? Didn't you feel the need particularly in your films that didn't have any strong narrative central line?

Ray, in close-up.

> RAY: It's all a matter of telling the story in the best possible way. If I had a complex kind of a story, which I had in certain films like *Days and Nights in the Forest* (*Aranyer Dinratri*) and *Kanchenjunga*, which are not at all conventional films, because they don't deal with one central character whom you follow or identify with. They are about a family or group of people where the story line is not really conventional.

A film clip from *Aparajito*, with a very ill Harihar lying unconscious in the foreground, and Sarbajaya fanning him with a palm-leaf fan. She turns her head to say something to Apu who is out of frame. He brings a brass pot of water which she tries to pour into his mouth.

RAY (*off*): But I have tried to keep the editing scheme as simple as possible, because I have a message to communicate also, but there are points where even as early as *Aparajito*, there were fairly bold cuts.

Cut to a close-up of the dying man's bulging eyes and the wife's hand pouring water into his mouth, till the neck suddenly goes limp, rolling the head back.

Cut to a pack of resting pigeons suddenly flying out, in semi-silhouette, as if frightened by some sudden happening.

Cut to another shot of the flying pigeons, fanning out in the sky.

SARBAJAYA (*off*): What is it? What has happened?

A man's hand wraps the mourning clothes around the young Apu's body, as camera tilts up to catch his still uncomprehending young face, his hair still wet from the dip in the holy Ganga.

Benegal, in close-up.

BENEGAL: A lot has been said about the way you use dialogue in your films, that it approximates closest to direct speech, and I'm told that this is very unusual in Bengali cinema. Is there . . . where did you get that from?

Ray, in close-up, in shirt sleeves.

RAY: Actually, as I told you earlier, I didn't have much confidence as a writer of dialogue when I started, but I was lucky to be using Bibhutibhushan's material—he wrote marvellous life-like speech, and I was able to lift the dialogue from the books and use in the films. But later on, when making

Jalsaghar, and particularly with *Parashpathar*, I started being creative as far as dialogue writing was concerned. And gradually what happened was that I wrote more and more a sparse kind of dialogue, which was a very functional kind of dialogue. As you probably know, a dialogue, apart from revealing characters, is also supposed to advance the story and give information, and all this.

BENEGAL (*off*): . . . and also humour.

RAY: . . . also humour, yes.

A film clip from *Shatranj he Khiladi* with Mirza Sajjad Ali reclining against a pillow, a chessboard laid out before him, and his chess-player friend, Meer Roshan Ali, rising to go into the inner chambers of the house.

MIRZA: Give my regards to the Begum Sahiba.

MEER: Don't fool around with those men behind my back.

Nafeesa, Meer's wife, and Aqil, Meer's nephew and Nafeesa's lover, sit close to each other on her bed, Aqil giving a demonstration of his skill at cracking his fingers. Nafeesa is full of admiration for her lover's genius.

NAFEESA: Oh wow! (*laughs.*)

They hear Meer approaching, humming a tune. The sound makes them start and jump out of the bed, Aqil rushing to hide under the bed.

But before Aqil can get under the bed, Meer is in the room, looking at Aqil on the floor, his expression registering incomprehension. What he sees is clear to the audience, although it does not appear in the frame.

Nafeesa, smart enough to invent a story, comes towards her husband, and puts her finger on her lips.

NAFEESA: Sh—h—h—h!

Aqil caught in an awkward position, half out and half in, does not know what to do.

Meer, uncomprehending, looks up at his wife, looking for an explanation.

As Aqil tries to scramble up to his feet, Nafeesa bends to push him down.

NAFEESA: No, no.

Close-up of Aqil, with Nafeesa's hand on his shoulder.

NAFEESA: Don't come out yet. It's not safe.

Meer looks in bewilderment at his wife and nephew, but cannot imagine what has been going on.

Close-up of Aqil, in the same awkward position.

Close-up of Meer.

MEER: What . . . ?

Nafeesa, in close-up, fumbles for words.

Meer, in close-up.

MEER: What is going on?

Nafeesa, in close-up.

NAFEESA: He . . . he is hiding.

Meer is still lost, for the obvious explanation does not enter his head. Nafeesa stands with her back to camera.

MEER: That I can see, but why?

Nafeesa, in close-up.

NAFEESA: They are after him.

Meer, still bewildered, with Nafeesa, back to camera.

MEER: Who is after him?

Aqil, in the same awkward position, half of his body still under the bed.

Meer, in close-up, notices a walking stick, hanging on a peg on the wall by its curved head.

MEER: Has he laid his hand on someone?

Meer's hand, in close-up, touches the walking stick, and a sword is partly unsheathed.

Meer, in close-up, taken aback.

MEER: What is this?

Nafeesa has run out of invention.

Meer faces the camera, with Nafeesa, her back to camera.

MEER: Why aren't you speaking?

Nafeesa, in close-up, silent.

Aqil, still in the same position.

Meer, waiting for an answer, gets impatient.

MEER: Are your lips glued? Why can't you tell me what has
    happened?

Aqil finds his voice at last.

AQIL: Nothing, sir.

Camera steals a quick glance at Nafeesa.

Meer faces the camera.

MEER: So who is after . . . ?

Nafeesa would like to give Aqil a little more time.

NAFEESA: Sh—h—h!

Meer lowers his voice immediately and joins in the game. He repeats
his question in a low voice this time.

MEER: Who is after him?

Aqil, unable to bear it any longer, comes out from under the bed,
and rises to his feet, at a little distance from Nafeesa, facing Meer
and the camera.

AQIL: The army.

The camera faces Meer, with Aqil, back to camera.

MEER: The army?

AQIL: Yes, sir.

MEER: Whose army?

Aqil stands at left of the frame, and Nafeesa at right, relieved at having found a story.

AQIL: Our army. The King's army.

NAFEESA: The King's army.

Meer, facing camera, and Aqil, back to camera.

MEER: Really?

AQIL: There may be a fight, Uncle, with the Company's army which has already come up to Kanpur.

Aqil and Nafeesa, facing camera, in medium shot.

AQIL: So the King's army is looking for men to become soldiers. They are short of men, you know.

NAFEESA: They have taken away a lot of men.

Meer, facing camera, in a shot taken from over the shoulder of Aqil.

MEER (*to Nafeesa*): You too know about this?

Aqil and Nafeesa face the camera again.

NAFEESA: Aqil was telling me just now.

Meer facing camera, in a shot taken from over the shoulder of Aqil.

AQIL: They are going from house to house. They went to our house too.

Nafeesa, right of frame, and Aqil, left of frame, face the camera as before.

NAFEESA: But he jumped to escape.

Meer, in close-up.

> MEER: I hope no one saw you running away.

Aqil and Nafeesa face the camera.

> AQIL: I don't know. They were on horseback. Two officers.
>
> NAFEESA: I think I too heard the sound of horse's hooves.

Meer, in close-up.

> MEER: When?

Aqil and Nafeesa, in medium shot, warm up to their story.

> NAFEESA: Just before you came in, clop-clop, clop-clop.

Close-up of Meer, who has obviously heard no such sound and is incredulous.

> MEER: But . . .

Aqil and Nafeesa wait to hear the verdict.

Something about the situation strikes Meer as odd.

> MEER: But why hide under the bed?

Aqil and Nafeesa have. no answer to this.

> MEER: Nobody can enter my inner chambers.

Aqil and Nafeesa, in close-up.

> NAFEESA: He lost his head.
>
> AQIL: I lost my head.
>
> NAFEESA: He's so timid, just like a child.

To convince Meer, Nafeesa takes his hand and places it on Aqil's chest, and keeps up her chatter.

NAFEESA: See, he is trembling all over, trembling like a leaf.

Meer is now convinced, and his expression changes to genuine concern.

MEER: Yes, I can see that. Give him a bowl of hot milk. Anyway, son, you're perfectly safe in my bedroom.

Medium shot of Aqil at right and Nafeesa left of frame, with Meer in the middle.

MEER: Perfectly safe . . .

With that he turns to go. They wait for him to be out of earshot, before they burst into laughter, and fall into each other's arms.

AQIL AND NAFEESA: Thank God.

Ray, in close-up.

RAY: So it was again a question of trying to be as economical as possible, while at the same time remembering the functions of a dialogue. And apart from that I suppose you have to have a good ear. You study the kinds of speech various kinds of people use, and . . .

Shyam Benegal, in close-up, nods in agreement.

RAY (off): . . . eventually use that in the film.

Ray, in close-up.

RAY: It's only while dealing with a village that one uses the convention of a roughly rural speech, without being consciously too regional, because that gives rise to all manner of problems with the actors. So in my Trilogy . . . well, I was using the speech Bibhutibhushan Bandyopadhyay had written. But even later for *Ashani Sanket* I had to fall back upon the kind of speech Bibhutibhushan had used, and this is accepted as rural speech.

Benegal, in close-up.

> BENEGAL: There is also another thing about your children's films. Now you've said of course that they are children's films for everybody, that doesn't exclude adult characters . . . You have this special way with children. But when you deal with adult characters in children's films, they also seem to assume childlike qualities. Is this your own sort of ideal, in your way of looking at the world?

Ray, in close-up.

> RAY: I don't think children's films call for child actors in them, they could well be about older people. Just as in *Goopy Gyne*, there are no children in *Goopy Gyne* at all, playing any leading part.

In a film clip from *Goopy Gyne and Bagha Byne*, Goopy and Bagha, the singer and the drummer, stand with folded palms in a space in eerie light suggesting the presence of the King of the Ghosts.

> RAY (*off*): These two are young men.

The King of Ghosts, with a star, made of flickering electric bulbs, behind him, bestows boons on Goopy and Bagha.

> THE KING: If you want food, you clap, clap, clap.
> If you want clothes, you clap, clap, clap.

Clap into each other's palms.
What other gift do you want?

The two friends, their palms still folded in salutation, are elated at their good fortune.

BAGHA (*stammering in excitement*): We . . . we love to travel.

GOOPY: If we could only travel!

The King of the Ghosts, against the flickering star.

THE KING: Well, well, well, you want to travel . . .

Two pairs of beautifully embroidered shoes appear before them from nowhere.

THE KING (*off*): These magic shoes you don,
Then clap into each other's palms.

Goopy and Bagha stare at him, finding it hard to believe their good fortune.

The King of the Ghosts smiles benignly at them.

Goopy and Bagha have now mustered enough courage and hope to ask for yet another gift.

GOOPY: If we could please people by the music we make!

The King of the Ghosts grants the gift with a gesture as he gradually recedes and finally disappears. The camera trolleys backwards letting the flickering star fade out in the distance.

Ray, in close-up.

RAY: There is *The Golden Fortress—Sonar Kella*—based on characters which I have created over the years, the detective and his young assistant . . .

The credits of *Sonar Kella*.

RAY (*off*): . . . and the original stories are all written from the point of view of this adolescent boy who is Watson to the Sherlock Holmes of Feluda, played by Soumitra.

In his grandfather's library, the boy mistaken for Mukul narrates his story, in a sequence from *Sonar Kella*, the camera facing the boy and his grandfather.

MUKUL: Phatik's House.

Feluda, at right of frame, with his young assistant, Topse, and Mukul's father between them, listens intently.

FELUDA: How did these two look?

Mukul and his grandfather face the camera.

MUKUL: They were bearded.

FELUDA: Both of them?

MUKUL: Yes. They said they were coming from Baluchistan.

GRANDFATHER: All rubbish.

Cut to Feluda.

FELUDA: Then?

Cut to the boy and his grandfather. The boy is obviously enjoying the importance he is receiving as a result of the kidnapper's mistake.

MUKUL: Then they clapped my mouth shut, bound my eyes up, and took me to a house. They asked me, 'Where is this golden fortress?' I said, 'I don't know, but Mukul does.' Then they asked me, 'What is your name?' I said, 'I am Mukul too.' Then they said, 'Mistake, mistake' in English, and asked me, 'Where is this other Mukul?' I said, 'He has left already.' They asked, 'For where?' I said, 'Jaipur'.

FELUDA: You said Jaipur?

The boy, standing, against a shelf loaded with books.

MUKUL: No, sorry. I said, Jodhpur. Then they gave me a glass of milk to drink. I told them that it was not the time I drank milk, but they forced my mouth open and poured it into it. Then I felt very sleepy.

Ray, in close-up.

BENEGAL (*off*): So far it appears that you have a preference for older writers, most of whom have written in the early years of the century. Of course you have made films from Sunil Ganguly's stories and so on . . . but do you have any special preference for that period of writing or some reason why you have done this over a period of time?

RAY: But again I have to work this out to find out if it is true. I mean, I've done Tagore three or four times. I've done Bibhutibhushan . . . well, the Trilogy itself . . . that's three films from one writer, then again *Ashani Sanket*. But there are a whole series of films which are by comparatively young writers. All the contemporary city stories are by Sunil, Shankar, or myself, I mean, *Kanchenjunga*.

The camera focuses on Ray's hand, in close-up, writing on paper clipped to a reclining board, then rises up his body, wrapped in a shawl, to his face in profile, a pipe held between his teeth.

> RAY (*off*): When I write original screenplays like *Nayak* or *Kanchenjunga*, I like to write about people that I know at first hand, who belong to the world I am familiar with— the middle class of today, the urban middle class, shall we say . . .

A medium shot of Ray at work, writing in the same posture, till the camera charges on his hand.

> RAY (*off*): I couldn't write about workers in a factory . . . I couldn't write. But I would like to make a film about workers in a factory.

Ray, in close-up.

> RAY: But for that I need material . . . I need a story for that, which I haven't found yet.

Ray, in close-up.

> BENEGAL (*off*): Now you have, say, written material or a short story that you might use, and then in adapting it, how much of your own experience would you put into it, for instance, into the script before you make a film of it?

> RAY: Well, I can't talk about experience, for that—because, well . . . the change varies from film to film . . . you do make changes . . . I mean in adapting a story for a film, for instance in *Pather Panchali*, it involved just cutting out characters . . . three hundred, I once counted about three hundred characters in the segment which I have used for the film. In my film there are about thirty. You have to cut

120

them out in a way that people are not aware of any essential things left out. But then with Tagore, for instance, some of the early short stories have a streak of sentimentality in them . . . a sort of Victorian attitude, and that I've had to change, to give it a more hard edge, a more contemporary kind of feeling. I had done that with the *Tin Kanya* stories, all of them. And later, with the contemporary stories, from the younger writers, I have . . . the changes have been called for, because sometimes the main character has changed, because in the process of preparing the script I have noticed flaws in the development of characters, what had struck me as flaws in adapting them, and their characters had to be given a more sort of logical development which has brought about changes in the structure of the story itself. So that has happened. These are basically . . . and sometimes you worked towards the conclusion . . . there is not a satisfactory conclusion to the original story.

Ray, in close-up.

RAY: You must have the feeling of doing the right thing in the right circumstances. And that comes from observation, your personal experience, although the story may be somebody else's. And there may be incidents which you have not experienced personally, directly. There is this thing like logic in a story which you . . . which makes your story ring true . . . whatever you make happen on the screen, you make ring true.

TITLE: ON FORM

Ray, in close-up.

RAY: In *Pratidwandi*, for instance, I used a lot of negative images, I think, in four or five different sequences . . . and it was dictated by . . . and I can tell you why I did it. Because the film starts with the scene of the boy's father dying, and his dead body being brought down the staircase, put on the floor, being garlanded, etc. . . .

An excerpt from Pratidwandi, entirely in negative, with a man holding up the curtain before a door to let a group of men carry a dead body out of doors.

RAY (*off*): Now I feel that if I had the normal positive image, people would look for signs of life immediately and it would be very difficult to make a convincing dead man.

In negative again, a close-up of the widow, weeping.

WIDOW: What'll happen to me?

A shot in the negative from the bottom of the staircase, as the men carry the dead body down, with the widow's sobbing continuing on the soundtrack.

WIDOW: Who else do I have?

Close up, of the widow, in negative.

Garlands on the dead man's face, in negative, from the perspective of someone standing at the head of the dead body.

A negative image of the son, standing pensively in front of the funeral pyre, till it gradually mixes to positive.

Ray, in close-up.

RAY: So since I had used negative in the opening sequences, I found reasons for using it as part of the language of the film in three or four other sequences.

Another sequence from *Pratidwandi*, with Siddhartha, the protagonist, in close-up, in negative.

RAY (*off*): So that is how that grew in that particular film.

In *Pratidwandi*, Siddhartha, in negative, lights a cigarette for the part-time prostitute that he visits with this friend. She bends over him in her bra to have the cigarette lit, and lets out a whiff of smoke in his face.

RAY: But generally I would say that I am not interested in form to begin with, that I am interested in the subject, and what interests me is density, how much can you tell, how telling can you make your images, and how much can you pack into a film without using gimmicks, or whatever you call them, wish to call them. Unconventional photographic or editing techniques . . . that sort of thing does not interest me to that extent. I think formally there are films I have made like *Kanchenjunga* and *Days and Nights in the Forest* which are quite original though they don't appear to be so, because the general storytelling is quite simple. But they grapple with a lot of things, a lot of characters and the attempt is to achieve clarity, with a group of characters, with a group of situations which don't follow a normal narrative pattern.

The elaborate memory game sequence from *Aranyer Dinratri*, with the group sitting on the grass in a circle.

JAYA: May I start?

SHEKHAR: Sure.

BENEGAL (*off*): Mr Ray has often referred to the influence of Western classical music on his work, Mozart's operas in particular. The ability of individual characters to maintain their individuality through elaborate ensembles. He says that the memory game in *Days and Nights in the Forest* attempts this. The game itself is the ground base over which the six characters play out their individual roles in word, look and gesture.

Close up of Jaya, starting the game with the name of her choice, and turning expectantly to the person next to her.

JAYA: Rabindranath.

The camera waits on Sanjay, who takes a little time before joining in.

SANJAY (*almost inaudible*): Karl Marx.

Aparna, in medium close shot. Benegal's words continue into this shot, overlapping her words.

APARNA: Cleopatra.

Camera focuses on Shekhar, with Aparna at right of frame, till it pans a little to bring Harinath in.

SHEKHAR: Wait. Rabindranath, Karl Marx, Cleopatra, Atulya Ghose. Hari, now it's your turn.

HARINATH: Rabindranath, Karl Marx, Cleopatra, Atulya Ghose.

SHEKHAR: What about yours?

HARINATH: Helen.

SHEKHAR: Helen of Troy, or Bombay?

HARINATH: Ugh! Bombay! (*He grimaces.*)

Aparna, in medium shot.

APARNA: OK, so it's Helen of Troy, very good.

Ashim at left of frame, with a part of the group, camera zooming in.

SHEKHAR: Ashim, your turn.

ASHIM: Rabindranath, Karl Marx, Cleopatra, Atulya Ghose, Helen of Troy. Shakespeare.

Aparna looks up at him with a smile.

Jaya's turn again, after the full circle has been covered.

JAYA: Oh, my God. I'm scared. Let me see . . . Rabindranath, Karl Marx, Cleopatra, Prafulla . . .

Shekhar jumps up at the mistake, and stops her before she can get the name out.

SHEKHAR: Out, Out.

Jaya, in medium shot, embarrassed.

JAYA: Oh shame! How could I make a mistake like that? It's Atulya.

It is Sanjay's turn. As he goes through the names, the camera moves from player to player, following Sanjay, out of frame now, looking at them one by one to recall the names that they had given, till it comes back to Sanjay.

SANJAY: Silence please. Don't confuse me. Rabindranath, Karl Marx, Cleopatra, Atulya Ghose, Helen of Troy, Shakespeare, out, Mao Zedong.

Aparna easily rattles off the names, not waiting to think, then adds her own choice.

> APARNA: Rabindranath, Karl Marx, Cleopatra, Atulya Ghose, Helen of Troy, Shakespeare, out, Mao Zedong, Don Bradman.

Shekhar's turn now. Hari smiles at him. Shekhar readies himself.

> SHEKHAR: It's my turn.

The whole group in long shot.

> SHEKHAR: Rabindranath, Karl Marx, Cleopatra, Atulya Ghose, Helen of Troy, Mao Zedong.

Jaya and Sanjay shoutout together.

> JAYA AND SANJAY: Wrong, wrong, out, out.

Shekhar, puzzled.

> SHEKHAR: What!

Sanjay smiles, in focus, before camera pans to Shekhar.

> SHEKHAR: Did I say Mao Zedong?

Shekhar, in uncertainty.

> SHEKHAR: What . . . what did I say?

Jaya, in medium shot.

> JAYA: Shakespeare.

Hari gets up nervously from his place in the circle, in long shot.

> HARI: I am not playing.

Shekhar, in the same long shot, turns to Hari.

SHEKHAR: Sit down, you. You've nothing else to do anyway.

Ashim in close-up, goes through the names correctly, with the camera moving over the others in accordance with the names that they had spoken.

ASHIM: Rabindranath, Karl Marx . . .

Ashim's voice, over the faces of the others, continues with the growing list accurately.

ASHIM: Cleopatra, Atulya Ghose, Helen of Troy, Shakespeare, out, Mao Zedong, Don Bradman, out, out, Rani Rashmoni.

Sanjay faces camera, with Aparna at left of frame, and Shekhar, with his back to camera.

SHEKHAR: Sanjay, show 'em.

SANJAY: Wait, let me see. Rabindranath, Karl Marx . . .

Sanjay fumbles after 'Mao Zedong'.

Jaya, in medium close shot, reclines on one elbow, a smile on her lips, waits for Sanjay to make a mistake.

JAYA: It's so easy. Can't you remember?

Aparna smiles at Sanjay's discomfiture.

Ashim, at left of frame, watches, with Hari, at right of frame, equally tense.

SHEKHAR (*off*): Isn't there any time limit in this game?

ASHIM: Yes, there is. Ten seconds.

Shekhar looks at his wrist watch.

SHEKHAR: I'll keep the time.

Jaya, at right of frame, waits with smile for the fall of Sanjay, left of frame, with his brows furrowed with intense concentration .

SHEKHAR (*off, counting*): One, two, three . . .

Shekhar finishes counting, and shouts.

SHEKHAR: Out, Out.

Jaya sits up, smiles.

JAYA: Bradman.

Camera focuses on Aparna, to whom the names come easily. She completes the list without a hitch and adds a new one.

APARNA: . . . Don Bradman, Rani Rashmoni, Kennedy.

Ashim, in focus.

ASHIM: Which Kennedy?

Aparna, in focus.

APARNA: Bobby.

Ashim in focus, about to join in.

Aparna, in focus, waits.

Focus on Ashim, as he concentrates and begins the list.

Jaya, in medium close shot, yawns and reclines on her elbow again, with Sanjay at left of frame.

Sanjay, in medium close shot, with Ashim's voice recalling the names.

SANJAY: Want a pillow?

Jaya, in focus.

JAYA: Do you have one?

Sanjay, in medium close shot, smiles.

SANJAY: Sure.

Jaya, in focus.

JAYA: Wait till he finishes.

The camera focuses on Ashim, as he completes the list.

ASHIM: Kennedy, Tekchand Thakur.

Aparna facing camera, in a shot taken from over the shoulder of Sanjay.

SANJAY: Shall be back in a minute.

APARNA: Sure. Rabindranath, Karl Marx . . .

Sanjay enters their room in the bungalow to collect a pillow for Jaya.

In a long shot, one notices two simple beds and a mirror hanging on the wall away from the camera. Sanjay, humming, picks up a pillow, stops at the door to come back and take a second pillow. He goes up to the door, steps back to look into the mirror and arrange his hair before he finally goes out.

Medium close shot of Jaya, reclining as before on one elbow. Sanjay offers her a pillow, from off the frame.

The camera pans to take Aparna in, almost at the end of her list. As she comes to the end of the list, there is a pillow for her too. She looks up, surprised.

ASHIM: Thank you.

The camera now goes back to the only other player left, Ashim, who starts the list all over again, with the camera panning to the reclining Jaya.

ASHIM: Rabindranath, Karl Marx . . . (*The voice fades in the distance.*)

JAYA (*to Sanjay*): Do you like Santali jewellery?

Sanjay, in focus, starts at the unexpected question.

SANJAY: Sorry?

JAYA (*off*): Santali jewellery. Do you like them?

SANJAY: On Santali women, definitely.

Jaya, reclining.

JAYA: I'll have to buy some for Mantu-di.

Ashim, in focus, coming to the end of the list.

Aparna, in focus, looking up as Ashim fumbles.

ASHIM (*off*): Kennedy.

Ashim, in close-up, trying hard to remember the next name.

ASHIM: Kennedy . . .

Shekhar, in focus, starts singing, jeeringly.

Ashim, in focus, obviously annoyed.

ASHIM: Oh, shut up.

Shekhar, in focus, makes a face. Jaya, in focus, makes a face.

Ashim, in focus, manages to remember the missing name, and carries on to the end of the list.

ASHIM: . . . Tekchand Thakur, Napoleon, Mumtaz Mahal.

Shekhar, in focus, is obviously envious.

SHEKHAR (*to Aparna*): Now it's your turn. Show him.

Aparna, in focus, looks up, smiles, and looks down.

Ashim, in focus, waiting for her to start and fail.

Aparna, in focus, smiles mysteriously.

APARNA: I don't think I can.

Jaya, in focus, reclining, surprised.

JAYA: Why?

Aparna smiles as before, but does not answer.

Jaya, in focus, sits up in utter surprise.

JAYA: You . . . you can't remember?

Aparna, with an inscrutable smile.

Shekhar, surprised.

Ashim, wondering.

Aparna smiles.

> APARNA: I think I now feel like Hari-babu . . .

Jaya is sure that Aparna remembers.

> JAYA: You don't remember the names from the beginning of the game . . . is that it?

Shekhar, in focus.

> SHEKHAR: Would you like to have some cold water from the well?

Aparna bursts out laughing, shaking her head.

Camera zooms to catch Ashim's expression. He has realized that Aparna has chosen to give up.

Aparna, in focus, looks up and smiles mysteriously.

> APARNA: No, I can't. Ashim-babu's the winner.

Benegal, in close-up.

> BENEGAL: You have always been an observer of, let's say, reality, if I might use the term, and whatever statements you have had to make have always been oblique.

Ray, in close-up.

> RAY: By temperament, I think I am a filmmaker who likes to be oblique, if such a thing is possible or valid in relation to the subject.

TITLE: APUR SANSAR

A film clip from *Apur Sansar*, with a view from the foot of the bed with two sleeping figures. As the alarm clock buzzes, Aparna wakes up and tries to clamber out of the bed.

She is held back by her sari stuck somewhere. She turns quizzingly. Apu is fast asleep with the end of Aparna's sari tied in a neat knot to the sheet that covers Apu.

Aparna unties the knot.

Close-up of Aparna's face, her hands and the knot.

Aparna slaps the sleeping Apu on the back playfully, then goes to the door, with the alarm still buzzing.

As the alarm stops buzzing, Apu wakes up, and turns his head slowly on the pillow to face the camera, smiling at sweet memories. He lifts a hair pin from near his pillow, obviously Aparna's, looks at it tenderly, yawns, and looks out of the room.

Apu's view of Aparna, in long shot, as she puts coal into the old-fashioned stove before lighting the fire for the day's cooking.

A closer view of the same scene.

Medium shot of Apu in bed.

Aparna looks at him, chides him on his behaviour, and goes back to work.

APARNA: What are you staring at me for? Am I new here?

Close-up of Apu bringing out a packet of cigarettes from under his pillow, as a train whistles by.

The packet of cigarettes, in close-up, revealing a message on the inside flap: 'Not more than one after every meal. Remember your promise?'

Apu looks at Aparna and smiles.

Aparna has watched the scene that brings a smile to her lips. Apu gives in with a smile, and puts the packet back under the pillow.

TITLE: ABHIJAAN

Camera in motion holds a field passing by, with a train on the horizon.

Close-up of an old man inside a car.
OLD MAN (FIRST PASSENGER): Isn't that our train?

Medium shot revealing three more passengers in the car, all of them old, rustic middle-class types.
SECOND PASSENGER: Yes, yes.
THIRD PASSENGER: That's right.

The first passenger, the old man, again.
FIRST PASSENGER: Yes, I'm sure it's our train, Singh-ji.

Singh-ji, the driver, a Sikh, with a severe expression, and a cigarette in his mouth, keeps on driving, without a reply.

FIRST PASSENGER (*off*): Are you sure you can reach us now? Singh-ji, sir?

Paddy fields, with a train on the distant horizon.

A low angle close-up of Singh-ji's assistant, hanging out from the car.

The engine driver looks at the car, which honks continuously.

The car racing through the fields, from the perspective of the engine driver.

A low angle shot of the engine driver smiling contemptuously at the car.

Singh-ji does not turn his head for a moment, but keeps an eye on the speeding train.

The train beyond the paddy fields.

Close-up of the engine driver, now tense and not smiling any more.

A close-up of Singh-ji's assistant, tense.

The old men in the car silent in their tension as they watch the car racing the train.

Singh-ji throws away his cigarette with a jerk, his only sign of excitement, as he continues driving, faster and faster, his eyes glancing sideways at the train.

The train is now closer, from the perspective of the car.

The car is closer, seen from the train.

The engine driver frowns as he feels the threat.

From the engine driver's point of view, the car comes closer.

Singh-ji, in close-up, tense.

The train, close by the car.

Singh-ji keeps an eye on the train, without turning his head.

Now the train is so close to the car that its passengers come into view.

Singh-ji's assistant bites his lips in excitement.

The wheel of the train, in close-up.

Singh-ji's profile, glancing at the train.

The train is so close now that one can read the number on the engine: BK 14.

The old passengers in the car wave a mocking goodbye to the train, as the car beats it in the race.

THE PASSENGERS IN THE CAR: Goodbye, goodbye.

The front of the engine recedes from the view of the passengers in the car.

TITLE: CHARULATA

A close-up of Charu's hands making a paan from the ingredients in her paan box.

Camera shifts from a close-up of Charu's face to her hands giving the final fold to the paan before she gets up from the bed and is about to go out of the room, but remembers something and turns towards the cupboard, which she opens to take out a pair of hand-made slippers.

Close-up of Amal, reading. As he hears Charu's footsteps, he rises to his feet and turns towards her.

Charu enters the room and comes up to him.

AMAL: *Bauthan*!

Charu, her back to the camera, practically pushes a paan lovingly into Amal's mouth.

Charu, now facing camera, thrusts the pair of slippers before Amal's eyes before placing them on the floor at his feet. Amal holds up the magazine he has been reading.

AMAL: You . . .

Charu snatches the magazine from his hand and throws it down on the floor.

AMAL: What are you doing?

Amal bends to retrieve the magazine which features a piece by Charu who turns and walks away to the window, as Amal addresses her.

AMAL: What's wrong with you? Do you have any idea of how well you have written? When I asked you to write about a village, I never imagined it would be so good—believe me!

Camera looks at Charu from the other side of the barred window, with Amal behind her at a distance. Her face shows no happiness. She turns towards Amal with a sob.

AMAL: I feel like a fool now. You write with such ease and so well. You mustn't stop. You must keep up your writing.

Charu comes up to him and breaks down into tears, as she places her face against his chest, with the camera zooming close to her.

CHARU: I won't write any more, I won't.

AMAL: Why are you crying?

She moves away from him, turns and goes back to the window again in an effort to control herself. Once she has been able to check herself, she comes back and fumbles with the objects on the table.

CHARU: I was a fool to cry.

She turns to leave the room, goes towards the door where she stops and comes back to Amal.

CHARU: Your shirt is wet.

She takes the magazine from him and goes out.

Title: Jana Aranya

The interior of a moving car, with the man driving it speaking to someone sitting next to him.

THE MAN: Blood sugar, high pressure, cholesterol . . . and my doctor is very strict.

The listener, in close-up, with a fixed smile on his lips.

A view of the street, seen through the front windscreen of the car.

With a close-up of the left front wheel in rotation, the car suddenly jumps at an obstruction on the road.

The glove case in front of the listener flies open, bringing into view a packet of cigarettes.

Close-up of the listener.

The listener's hand, in close-up, puts the lid back on the glove case.

The rotating wheel again, and the car jumps, while the man continues his monologue.

THE LISTENER (off): Honestly? You don't smoke? You must be . . .

The listener, smiling, in close-up.

THE MAN (off): I don't smoke, because I am scared of contracting cancer.

Close-up of the listener, obviously taken aback at this blatant lie.

Close-up of his hand rotating on the lid of the glove case.

TITLE: PIKOO

In a colourful outdoor scene, a bush of white flowers, Pikoo with his drawing book, and a glimpse of the balcony of his mother's bedroom. The balcony has a deserted look, with the curtains drawn over the windows behind it.

Pikoo looks up at the balcony.

> PIKOO (*shouts*): Ma!

Inside the mother's bedroom, the mother and her lover are in bed together, their shoulders uncovered. Pikoo's call interrupts their love making, and they look towards the camera, listening.

Pikoo in the garden.

> PIKOO: Ma!

Close-up of the face of Hitesh, his mother's lover.

A close-up of the lovers in bed, with Hitesh trying to pull her back to the act, as she turns her face back in the direction of the voice.

Top shot of the small boy, alone in the garden, looking up, and shouting.

> PIKOO: I'm drawing white flowers in black because I have no white crayons.

Hitesh, in close-up, tries to pull her back.

Close-up of Hitesh, his face hardening.

In close-up, Hitesh tries again.

In close-up, Hitesh's angry face, as he gets up.

In close-up, an open page of a drawing book with a child's hand drawing a flower, till a raindrop falls on the drawing, smudging it at once.

In a medium close shot, Pikoo makes a face.

A carpeted staircase, in long shot, with the boy running up the stairs, shot from the bottom of the staircase.

A top shot of the staircase, with Pikoo turning around the bend of the staircase.

In a long shot, he crosses the hall, heading towards his mother's room.

As Pikoo enters the left end of the corridor, he can hear the voices of his mother and her lover quarrelling behind the closed door of his mother's bedroom.

    PIKOO'S MOTHER (*off*): I have told you.

    HITESH (*off*): What have you told me?

    PIKOO'S MOTHER (*off*): I have told you I am sorry.

    HITESH (*off*): How does that help?

The closed door.

    PIKOO'S MOTHER (*off*): You are behaving as if . . .

Pikoo slowly advances towards the closed door.

    PIKOO'S MOTHER (*off*): . . . it happens every day.

    HITESH (*off*): From now on it'll happen every day. You should've
        told me that I shouldn't come today, that it'd be inconven-
        ient.

    PIKOO'S MOTHER (*off*): Won't you come any more?

    HITESH (*off*): Oh! I've learnt my lesson.

    PIKOO (*shouting at the top of his voice*): Shut up!

He smiles as the quarrelling stops at once.

Long shot of the corridor, with the child running towards his grandfather's room.

    PIKOO: Grandpa!

Close-up of the stiffened hand of his grandfather, as he lies dead in
his bed. The child's hand feels his pulse.

Close-up of Pikoo, realizing that his grandfather is dead, as music
starts on the soundtrack.

The dead grandfather in his bed, with his bedside table full of bottles
and phials, as the music continues.

A close shot of a cane chair on the corridor, with Pikoo coming into
the frame and slowly sitting down in it, against the sound of thunder
on the soundtrack.

A vase with a solitary pink flower, against the sound of a car starting and driving off.

Close-up of Pikoo, in profile, sobbing silently, as he stares at the vase.

Close-up of the drawing book and the pen set lying on his lap. His hand takes a pen out of the set.

Pikoo looks up at the sound of a door opening, as he takes the pen out.

In a long shot, the door at the far end of the corridor opens to bring his mother into view, in silhouette against the window lights.

Pikoo, in close-up, looks straight in front of him, at the flower—not at his mother, nor in the direction where his grandfather lies dead.

Close-up of the pink flower in the vase.

Close-up of Pikoo, sniffing, with tears in his eyes, as he concentrates on drawing the flower.

Ray, in close-up.

>   BENEGAL (*off*): Well, for many years you have been . . . you know . . . your status in Indian film has been, as one might call it, one of splendid isolation. You have been quite alone in what you have been doing, and with the kind of concern you show in your films. Now, has that affected you in any way, because there hasn't been enough of a kind of a bouncing board to react against or to place yourself in the milieu?

RAY: Well, this is not something of my creation. I mean one would have wanted, for instance, to start a trend, a whole new trend or something like that. But we have had directors here in Bengal—a couple of directors here certainly who have been working almost simultaneously with me. They started at about the same time as I did, Ritwik and Mrinal. They were both working, not Ritwik so much, but Mrinal worked fairly regularly, and then Ritwik off and on. They were making films very different from mine, very different, but very powerful, I think. So in any case filmmaking has so many hassles that . . . so problematic here to get a film done . . . one stops thinking whether you are creating a school or whether others are following in your footsteps. You just keep on working because after all it's also a living, and you make a living, and you express yourself at the same time, crossing many obstacles on the way. Filmmaking has never been easy here. Certainly not.

BENEGAL (*off*): But doesn't it . . . don't you feel the need that you do require a kind of stimulus, outside the one that you generate for yourself as a filmmaker?

RAY: What stimulus are you talking about? Because by and large my films, many of my films, have been received well, for instance, if not here . . . sometimes here, sometimes abroad. So there has been a sense of satisfaction after making a film. Nothing, almost nothing, with the exception of two or three which either didn't export or didn't go down well here, most of the films have eventually had success, been successful in the sense that they have got either money or recognition. Almost none of my films has lost money. Eventually, in course of time, they have brought back their cost. So it's been more or less . . . the feeling has been a fairly happy one. But the difficult part has been the making of it.

Ray, in close-up.

> RAY: It takes a long time to . . . (*pause.*) . . . gauge an audience.
> You know, one makes a film with a sort of ideal audience
> in mind. One hopes that one can do what one likes oneself,
> gets excited about it . . . finds it absorbing . . . hopes there
> will be an audience to have the same sort of reaction to the
> film once it is made. But in the earlier stages, I think I made
> many mistakes, because, for instance, *Pather Panchali* was
> a great success, *Aparajito* was not. It was a failure from the
> box office point of view, and that applies to *Aparajito* all
> over the world, it is the same reaction everywhere, which
> is very interesting, because you obviously have a kind of
> standard general audience reaction to a film regardless of
> where the audience is. But watching the film with the audi-
> ence one realizes that there are mistakes in the film, and
> the mistake is not perhaps in the audience, but in the maker.
> Since I have tried not to repeat myself, there has been an
> element of risk in almost everything I have done because I
> was trying out something new, something which the audi-
> ence had not seen before. So it has been like that, and also
> the fact is that the audience has grown over the years, has
> become more mature, more sophisticated over the years.
> Partly from the film society movement, partly from the
> fact that seeing my latest film has been a sort of necessary
> cultural sort of necessity, and they have followed my trend
> very very carefully. I am talking only of the urban audiences.
> I don't really know what happens outside the city limits.

Ray, in close-up.

RAY: May have had something to do with what I inherited from my family, my father's side, mother's side.

BENEGAL (*off*): Because it also reflects a very strong rationalist kind of streak?

RAY: Yes.

BENEGAL (*off*): Which also to some extent might be your Brahmo upbringing?

RAY: Could be. Although one is not conscious of it, because we were born Brahmos. You know, actually the conversion had taken place much earlier. So naturally from my household I was imbibing certain values, a certain attitude, even from childhood when one was not doing it consciously. But it was just there. It was just things that we observed and learnt through observation. Must have been there.

BENEGAL (*off*): When did you start to feel being affected by your environment? At what stage in your life were you looking at life and relating to other people? Let us say, for instance, the problems of the city of Calcutta itself.

RAY: Well, as an illustrator—I was an illustrator before I was a filmmaker—as an illustrator, one has to be very observant, observing people's behaviour. When you illustrate, when you are a realistic kind of illustrator, which I was—I have also done a lot of stylized work but there was a lot of realistic illustration work which calls for a great deal of observation of people's behaviour, physical types, and environment, and this and that, so *that* had already happened even during my advertising days.

TITLE: ON ANGER AND IRONY

Ray, in close-up.

>RAY: I think there is anger when it is called for, or anger is needed, as you will probably find in my latest film. About the other thing, as you say, I have converted it into irony. It is something that came from a remark which my teacher, Nandalal Bose, made in Santiniketan. He once said—apropos what I have forgotten—he said, there are two kinds of people. One, the very angry people, who give vent to their anger. But he said, I feel the stronger person is the angry man who can control his anger, stronger than the person who gives vent to his anger. That struck me as an interesting remark. And irony has of course appealed to me all along, I think. Why I can't say . . . perhaps because life itself is ironic, when you juxtapose it with death, you know.

The final shot of the film is from outside the building in which Ray has a second floor flat. Through a lighted window one can see Ray in profile, smoking a pipe and maybe writing. The camera slowly zooms back from there to hold the whole house in darkness, with the sky above, with the two lighted windows standing out.

The last credits and acknowledgements, set in Ray Roman, come against a piece of music from a Tagore song, used in *Charulata*— *Mama chittey niti nrityey* (In my heart there dances eternally . . .).

Conversations

Shyam Benegal was kind enough to hand over to us a complete tran-
script of his 'conversations' with Satyajit Ray. What follows is an
edited and tidied up selection from material that has not gone into
the film proper. Quite a large part of this represents a director
exchanging notes with another director—not necessarily meant for
the consumption of the public, and hence maybe more full of insights.

SAMIK BANDYOPADHYAY

The Beginning

BENEGAL: Mr Ray, why did you start making films and what made you start making films?

RAY: I was, as you probably know, in advertising. In fact, I was in advertising even when I made *Pather Panchali*, I still had my job. But I was, as you know, deeply involved, not in the making of films, but in the study of films. We had started this film club in 1947, and I was an avid moviegoer, and I was reading a lot on cinema, all aspects of it, and I was getting a little tired of advertising as a profession, and the ethics of advertising. The fact that you had to contend with clients and all that didn't make me very happy, till there came a point where I decided that I'll try and change my profession. But I couldn't afford to leave my profession at the time when I made my first film, because part of my salary went into the making of the film, so that I was shooting over weekends and holidays.

BENEGAL: But why film? Weren't you a painter?

RAY: Yes, I was a painter, but cinema seemed a far more exciting kind of medium. Cinema, not painting, was really my first love. I never called myself a painter. I was taught as a painter in Santiniketan, where I studied fine arts, but then I went into advertising art, and got involved with a publisher, doing book jackets and photography. But the first interest was cinema all along.

The Apu Trilogy

BENEGAL: A very interesting element in your early work—in the Apu Trilogy, for instance—is the use of details, not just in terms of information, but in terms of their ability to *express*, a detail revealing a great deal of things—relationships between people, states of mind, states of emotion—marvellous examples, almost as though you have used it as language in cinema. But then in the later films, slowly you're no longer using that kind of vocabulary.

RAY: Well, I think that the trilogy stories needed details because from the narrative point of view there wasn't that kind of strength of appearance as you'd find in a normal screenplay. These are more sort of lifelike fragments, you know, so that they have to be made effective by means of details. Some of the details come from Bibhutibhushan Banerjee, some of them come from the European cinema which I admired. Details have been part of most of my films, but not perhaps to the extent they were used in the trilogy. Bibhutibhushan himself was fond of details of that nature, and I am very fond of details myself.

BENEGAL: In *Apur Sansar* you had a much stronger narrative line than the first two parts of the trilogy. It has a kind of movement—while the other two films have exceedingly short scenes put together, *Apur Sansar* has longer scenes. There is a story movement that is evident. How did it happen?

RAY: Well, for one thing it was difficult to find a clear narrative line in the first two parts. For another, by the time of *Apur Sansar* I had learnt to write a scenario and structure a film. In fact *Apur Sansar* is more me than the other films in the trilogy, although the main events, even in *Apur Sansar*, come from the book itself—like the death at childbirth, Apu leaving the son and then coming back and finding him again—all those sort of crucial points, the turning points, are there in the original book, but the structuring—for the structuring I used a lot of my own experience. It was a properly developed scenario.

BENEGAL: I see. There is another very interesting thing about the trilogy. As it deals with a village and eventually with the city, it appears to be in some ways a kind of idealization of a certain way of life, a certain kind of living, it also sort of stresses that there is a certain kind of harmony accommodating a whole natural order of things.

RAY: That's very much Bibhutibhushan, and I wanted to stick to it. I wanted to stick to the philosophy of the book, to his attitude to life. That is very much Bibhutibhushan.

BENEGAL: Do you agree with that yourself?

RAY: I did agree. Certainly at that point it seemed right for the three films.

BENEGAL: You didn't wish to editorialize or comment on it in any of the three films?

RAY: No, not at that point. No, certainly not.

BENEGAL: There is another thing in the trilogy. Apu growing up in this village, being part of that situation, and eventually breaking out of it, and that, you know, happens because of his Western education.

RAY: Yes. That is the point that he makes, and I felt that it was absolutely right, it had to be emphasized, it had to be kept, and also his growing up and away from his mother, which was strongly criticized in Bengal, as being wrong.

BENEGAL: But isn't there also a kind of confronting position arrived at on one level, if you look at it philosophically? There's the question of this whole natural order of things, with acceptance as way of life, and suddenly one person breaks out of it. And then it seems to be done so very painlessly. But do you yourself see it happening in the same way in life?

RAY: Well, perhaps not today to that extent. But don't forget that this deals with an earlier Bengal. The book came out in the 1930s, and Bibhutibhushan was talking about his own childhood and his own manhood eventually. So it was all very turn of the century, and I saw no sense in departing from Bibhutibhushan's conception of life.

BENEGAL: But do you yourself sort of feel comfortable with the sense of order you like in . . . ?

RAY: I did. I did at that point. It felt right. To me it felt right.

BENEGAL: Yes.

RAY: In the two stories, in the three films, there are pretty harsh, really harsh things—the death of the old woman, the death of the father, all those things that are shown there in a fair amount of brutal details.

BENEGAL: But don't you see that death is never there, and there is no sense of horror about death for instance? It seems like you accepted this whole process. If you take the choice of subjects even after the trilogy, what you have chosen always appear to relate somehow to an attitude of accepting the natural order of things. Do you feel most comfortable with subjects of that kind when you make films?

RAY: I think it applies more to my early films than the later ones. I think I have changed directions, even if imperceptibly, over the years—occasionally, certainly. But I certainly felt very comfortable with the material which I got from Bibhutibhushan's two novels, and I had no doubts when making the trilogy as to what I was, you know, what I wanted to say, and how I said it, and how much it was all related to the original book. In fact, I was trying to stick very closely to the spirit of the two books, and I think, to a certain extent, I did succeed.

BENEGAL: After the trilogy, after the Bibhutibhushan novels, you went on to Tagore.

RAY: Yes, I did. One of the reasons was that it was Tagore's centenary that year.

BENEGAL: But do you now feel that at that time that was the real reason?

RAY: Certainly. I was asked to make a documentary on Tagore, and I wanted to pay a sort of personal tribute. And I had been wanting to . . . I have always admired his short stories. Many of his short stories are not expandable. So I decided, why not make a package of three short stories, and keep them short, that was the idea. A personal tribute to Tagore, a sort of a centenary tribute.

BENEGAL: Then you made *Charulata*.

RAY: Not after that. That was three films after that.

BENEGAL: But do you identify with Tagore in any way?

RAY: Well, certainly. Some of his things, I do identify very strongly with. He was far ahead of his times. We looked up to him and we admired him—as a musician and as a writer of short stories. Some of his novels too I greatly admired. *Charulata* is not a novel however, it's a short story really.

BENEGAL: The reason I ask you this question is that Tagore was a multifaceted personality, a Renaissance man. You have a great many interests yourself. You are interested in painting and music and cinema and literature. You do several things. Is that why you feel greatly at home with Tagore?

RAY: Well, I don't know. If you are talking about versatility, it runs in the family. My grandfather was a similar kind, a many-sided genius. He was painter, musician, poet, photographer, block-maker, scientist, astronomer. So was my father, except that he died very young. In his short life, he wrote, he painted, and, well, he was very versatile, and I have never thought in terms of identifying with Tagore, except that we all—most Bengalis, every educated Bengali—admire him tremendously as a giant among Bengalis, a multifaceted genius.

BENEGAL: Yes, but wouldn't there be as one aspect of it an evaluation of Tagore from contemporary sensibility?

RAY: Yes, it could happen maybe in turning his stories into films. I was not doing them slavishly, there was a considerable amount of bringing them up to date, in the sense that I myself as a film-maker was viewing the stories from my contemporary point of view. All the stories, if you compare them with the originals, are considerably adapted, they are just not exact replicas of the originals.

Beyond the Trilogy

BENEGAL: Did you ever think of adding another film to the trilogy?

RAY: No.

BENEGAL: With Apu as father?

RAY: No, not really. But in the third part of course he grows up. Then you have another Apu. No, another film would have been too much. This is right. In fact, he comes back to life at the end, which he doesn't in the book, where he again becomes vacant and goes on wandering, leaving Kajal alone. I thought it needed a positive ending after all the deaths and tragedies and separations and what not.

BENEGAL: There is a point of view that the film could easily have ended with his throwing away of the novel . . .

RAY: Oh, there!

BENEGAL: . . . you know when.

RAY: But I think one would have wanted to know what happened to the child. It was very necessary, it was obligatory to bring the child in, and bring the father back to the child, and have the father take the responsibility of bringing up the child. I think that was my view, and it was a long, long film if you conceive it in terms of one single unit, and then it needed that positive ending, a jubilant kind of ending.

Music

BENEGAL: When you started, your music was very different from the way it was being used in Indian films. You developed a very strong thematic score, you had a very strong thematic line running throughout the trilogy, and you used music also in dramatic ways which were much more conventional, underlining emotional moments, anticipating, and so on. But over a period of time, you have given up the use of dramatic music, and you do use thematic lines, but often even not that.

RAY: Yes. Well, in the beginning, I had no confidence in myself as a composer. Of course I was very aware of music in films, and there were certain basic instructions always given to the composers I worked with, like having certain themes for certain situations or for entire films. *Pather Panchali* had such a theme which recurred seven or eight times in the film. Ravi Shankar had the theme in mind even before he saw the film. He hummed it to me, I said it was marvellous and this would go very well with the film. It comes back at certain points, and gives it a unity, because, if you are using a new piece of music every time, it doesn't work, because the audience is also looking at the images, following the story, listening to the dialogue—and the music is lost generally if it's a new piece every time. So unless the piece of music recurs at least three or four times in a film one doesn't remember it, one doesn't know it, and one doesn't connect it with the film, and it doesn't become part of the film. In the early films and also in the period films, we moved away from our own time, so they were on a slightly different level, and we had to have more music. Ali Akbar working on *Devi* or Ravi Shankar on the trilogy, or Vilayat on *Jalsaghar* always provided me with quite an amount of music which was used in the films. But later I took over composing myself because for one reason they were not available half the time, as they were on tours, and by that time I had acquired a certain degree of confidence as a composer myself; and in any case even at the beginning I was getting ideas of my own and it was often not very convenient to be dictating, telling them what to do. They had to be left there to their own devices to a certain extent. So music in the trilogy takes a big part, and is, as you say, both incidental and dramatic, underlining certain emotions. But this business of underlining—in fact the films of the thirties and the forties, the American films, that we admired in those days, were often drowned in music—I never liked, you know. Some of the European directors making films in America opened my eyes to the other kind or use of music—like the first film of Jean Renoir that I saw, *The Southerner*, which had very little music, but had a rich soundtrack. That I saw some time in 1944 or 1945. So that was the model for me. Music when it is a must, but again one uses it with the audience in mind, when you think perhaps they would not be able to get the meaning, the emotional content of the scene. So you underline it. That I have done. But the thematic music that gives the film unity, that also is a very important element which I still keep using, when I'm using music. But sometimes they are just effects, or very close to effects, not necessarily melodic, linear melodic music.

BENEGAL: And you seem to be doing more of that now than . . .

RAY: Yes, I'm trying to be economical with music.

BENEGAL: Do you write your own scores?

RAY: Yes, I do.

BENEGAL: Wouldn't you be able now to use a composer for your films, where your ideas can be conveyed to him and he could work out a score?

RAY: Well, the ideas now would be in the nature of actual lines of melody with the orchestral colour and everything. So why? If one uses a composer one has to give him a certain degree of freedom, and there's always a possibility that he will provide me with something which I don't like. And then there will be clashes, and this and that.

BENEGAL: Yes.

RAY: So I have avoided that more or less.

BENEGAL: How did you come to music initially?

RAY: I was surrounded by music. Everybody on my mother's side could sing, all my aunts, all my uncles, my mother was an exceptional singer. It was mainly Rabindrasangeet, Tagore's songs, that I heard as a child, and the Brahmo Samaj songs—some of them are wonderful, really magnificent songs based on classical ragas, and those I remember very well. As I said, music was all around. Of course, I never heard my grandfather play the violin, but I'm told that he was exceptional. Music, I never studied. It *was* just with me all along. Towards the end of my school days, I became interested in Western Classical music. Some years later there was a gramophone club in Calcutta, and we became members. By that time I had started buying miniature scores.

There would be mainly Parsis really, and some foreigners who were still in town. There were very few Bengalis really. There was a Calcutta Symphony Orchestra. I started going to the concerts of this orchestra. Nirad Chaudhury was one of the few Bengalis who used to go to those concerts. I took my collection of records with me to Santiniketan, where the one big advantage was that there was a Professor of English or Comparative Literature, a German Jew called Dr Aronson, and he had his own collection of records. We used to listen to music every evening in his house. He had his gramophone. And he played the piano. There was a piano in Uttarayan in Santiniketan—in the building where Tagore lived. Aronson lived in one of the smaller houses, but in the big house there was a piano, not very well tuned, but he used to go there and play the piano. I persuaded him to play the piano for me, and I turned the pages for him. So that was one additional thing which made me familiar with Western notation. So throughout my Santiniketan days I was pursuing music, along with painting.

BENEGAL: But when you were in college did you find friends who shared your interests?

RAY: Well, there was one friend—yes, I did have one friend—who certainly shared my interest in music, and Western classical music. And he kept it up even after college—he was quite wealthy certainly, much more affluent than I was. He built up a huge collection of records quite early on, he could afford it. He had a very big radio, and used to listen to foreign broadcasts of music, particularly the German stations were very powerful. It was the Nazi year, and you could hear a lot of good music at the time.

BENEGAL: Was there nobody at all besides him?

RAY: No, there was nobody, certainly not in the early stages. Later there were others. But in the early stages I was certainly very much alone, going to the record shops, just rummaging through their collection. Then there was a point when I found that there weren't that many records of classical music on the catalogue. I started corresponding with the Gramophone Company manager. He was an Englishman. Then I suggested they bring out regular issues of classical music in Calcutta, because there were people interested. Not that I knew very many who were interested, but I had to tell this little lie. Anyway he reacted very favourably, and I had in fact given him a list of classics which I felt would be right for Calcutta, and then they did manage to bring them out eventually.

BENEGAL: It was a kind of lone quest?

RAY: It was a lone quest, very much a lone quest. I started building up my collection of records. At first I could afford only one movement a month maybe, so it took about three months to build a symphony or a concerto. But later on, when I had my job, it was a little easier on the finances.

The Other Arts—and Cinema

BENEGAL: When would you say you had your first exposure to art, say the art of the world, not just Indian art or music?

RAY: Well, I would say it all happened at Santiniketan, within the three years that I was there. We had a magnificent library, and I had a couple of friends. One is now a celebrated Professor of Indian art in Hawaii. We became very close friends, and he had a fantastic knowledge of art—world art—and great perception and sensitivity. So I came under his influence at that time. As a student of painting he had as much to teach me as the professors of Santiniketan really.

161

BENEGAL: And your interest in the cinema. When did that start?

RAY: Well, it's very hard to say when it started, because I remember being a film fan as a very small boy, and even early in the school years, I used to buy magazines like *Picturegoer* and *Film Pictorial*, and I had my own star rating system. I used to keep notes of the films I would see, and give them ratings, my own sort of ratings in stars. So it started as a kind of interest in film stars, and then the films along with the stars. But the interest in the directors came later, I think in the early days of college . . . I became conscious of the cinema bearing the stamp of its own maker. Then again things happened in Santiniketan, where I was helped by the fact that there were in the library, which consisted mainly of books on art and painting, some film books. You know, the standard film books—like Pudovkin's *Acting and Film Technique*, and Rotha's *Film Till Now*. Those two or three books I read again and again. That made me conscious of cinema as an art form, the narrative styles that one uses—terms like close-ups and long shots, trolleying, and cuts and fades and what not, and dissolves.

BENEGAL: Were you fond of certain kinds of films?

RAY: Well, I think when we were very young, we were allowed to see a certain kind of films, because our parents and elders usually told us what we should see. So in the very early days it was things like *Robin Hood* and *The Count of Monte Cristo*, and that sort of thing. Later on, I think when I was nine or ten, in the early days of sound, mind you, that would be the thirties, the very early thirties, I remember seeing the early Lubitsches, nearly all of them, with Maurice Chevalier, you remember, and Janet Macdonald, *Love Parade*, *Smiling Lieutenant*, and all those Lubitsch films I remember exceedingly well. So they must have made a very strong impression. Not the stars so much as the way of telling the story, the witty kind of things that Lubitsch was doing all the time.

FIGURES 59–62. Posters designed by Ray for his films (*clockwise*): *Devi* (1960, *Pratidwandi* (1970), *Apur Sansar* (1959) and *Parashpathar* (1957)

FIGURE 63. Back to the beginnings: Chidananda Dasgupta speaking at a Calcutta Film Society reception for Pudovkin and Cherkasov

FIGURE 64. Catching up with the past, with Frank Capra at Delhi at the international film festival: 'I was reading up on people like Capra, and looking for their sort of special characteristics.'

FIGURES 65–66. Ray shooting *Aranyer Dinratri* (*top*); and *The Inner Eye*, with the painter Benode Behari Mukherjee (*bottom*).

FIGURES 67–68. Ray with his contemporaries: with Antonioni and Kurosawa before the *Taj Mahal* (*top*) and with Bergman (*bottom*).

BENEGAL: What about Westerns?

RAY: Westerns, yes, but not to the same extent. When I really got interested in Westerns, but that time I was already very seriously interested in cinema, and so I was looking for John Ford and William Wyler and things like that.

BENEGAL: What about Indian films? Bengali and Hindi films?

RAY: No, really. I think we avoided them as much as possible. Well, there were relations working in the cinema. I had an uncle who was one of the major directors, Nitin Bose at New Theatres. His brother, Mukul Bose, was the audiographer or the sound record-ist, as they say. They were both very talented, particularly from the technical point of view. So we inevitably saw their films in those days, and I could see that they were well photographed and that the sound recording was of a high calibre. But I was never interested in the stories or the way they were told. It was a strange concoction. They seemed to stick to a formula even in those days. So I wasn't looking at the Indian films really for any kind of real edification or education. They were there, they had to be seen occasionally, but the real interest was in foreign films. And foreign films usually meant American films in those days.

BENEGAL: Were you aware of the work Prabhat was doing, for instance?

RAY: Not really, not before we started our film society. I knew there was somebody called Shantaram, and there was a Prabhat Studio, and they were turning out big films, ambitious films. But it was only after we formed the film club that we deliberately got films from the Prabhat period and showed them to the members, and we were impressed by them. Some of them, and *Ramshastri* in particular, I remember. I don't know whether that was a Prabhat film but that was certainly one of the Marathi films that seemed like a very serious effort, and impressive.

BENEGAL: When did you, I mean, what motivated you to start the Calcutta Film Society?

RAY: Aw, just that it was a big thing in Europe. I think I found a lot of young people who shared my interest in the cinema. And it just came up one evening while we were sitting and chatting—'Why don't we start a film society?'—there were Chidananda Dasgupta and three or four others—and it was 'OK, let's get going.' That's how it happened. When it did happen we were all very serious. We started a library of film books, we had seminars and discussions. When Renoir came to Calcutta to shoot *The River*, we invited him, and he gave a talk. Verrier Elwin gave a talk. Soon after we formed the film society in 1947, we were lucky to have some celebrated filmmakers and film actors arriving in Calcutta from abroad. Pudovkin and Cherkasov came as part of a delegation. They came with some films, and they gave talks. We also had showings of films like *Ivan the Terrible* and some of the early Pudovkin classics. We were quite active in the early days.

BENEGAL: When did you first get to know films other than American films?

RAY: When I went to London, in 1950.

BENEGAL: What was the impact of that when you first saw . . . ?

RAY: Oh, that was fantastic. Actually I had gone to work in the head office of my British advertising agency. But my wife and I immediately became, as soon as we arrived, members of the London film club. They had a Marx Brothers season on. And we were living at Hampstead right close to Everyman's Cinema which was a sort of a permanent film festival. And so in the space of four and a half months we saw something like a hundred films. The neorealists had just come up, you know. *The Bicycle Thieves*. Italian films, French films, German films, we were seeing all, we were just lapping them up.

The Making of a Film

BENEGAL: How much of a film of yours, once you've worked out the sequence or the sequences within the film, is improvised by way of breaking down shots, or . . . ?

RAY: Well, I seldom depart from the master plan. There's never getting away from the total structure which is very firmly in my head. But within that structure there is a considerable lot of things that are improvised at the shooting stage . . . changes of angles, a little business, the dialogue for instance is constantly being pruned—I mean, I've written the dialogue, the actress has learnt the lines, but at the time of rehearsal perhaps I feel that I can prompt three words there or an entire sentence perhaps, and use it, just for instance . . .

BENEGAL: Oh no, what I meant was, for instance, in the change of angles.

RAY: Oh, yes.

BENEGAL: You might work out a different set of angles, you might break down a scene differently from what you had conceived on paper.

RAY: Yes, that also is done occasionally, particularly in scenes of dialogue where two or three persons are speaking. I have the alternatives to break it up, to take it in one shot, to break it up into overhead shots, and things like that. After the rehearsals, you often have ideas which you try to incorporate.

BENEGAL: Do you try to change in the editing stage?

RAY: In the editing stage I never look at the script. I look at the material of the shot, and I get ideas from that. They even lead to conclusions where you might want a new shot, perhaps you want to add something. But I never look at the script again. I only look at my shots.

The Later Films

BENEGAL: I have an elaborate question now. In your rural films you have a central character with a quality of innocence about him. But when you come to the urban films there suddenly appears to be a loss of such innocence. When I saw *Pratidwandi* for instance, it represented to me that loss of innocence, and then it is carried on in *Jana Aranya* and several other films you have made since and even before that. Is this your own world view? Is it your view that rural life is basically innocent and in urban life there is a process of a loss of innocence?

RAY: That would apply certainly to the films that I have made on rural life, except *Ashani Sanket*, where you have this brahman character who is in a way quite worldly wise, in a way quite clever and resourceful. But that's different from the city kind of resourcefulness or vanity or sophistication. And when I have dealt with urban characters they have mainly been the literate middle class or even the slightly upper class. So naturally it would be true to life to make them aware, that's all.

BENEGAL: But is it only awareness, for there also appears to be a breakdown somewhere of a whole set of moral values?

RAY: Yes, but that is because I've chosen that kind of a story to show a certain aspect of society, and that has been the theme of the films, particularly *Jana Aranya* or even *Seemabaddha* or *The Adversary*. So it had to be part of the film, had to be part of the attitude.

BENEGAL: But does that reflect your own view?

RAY: Obviously I was sympathetic to these views. Otherwise I wouldn't have made the films.

BENEGAL: But now when you proceed further—for instance, you mentioned how in the late sixties and early seventies you were passing through a process of revaluating and reassuring your attitude about your own environment—has that been continually reflected in your work, or in the way you think about films?

RAY: Up to a point, yes. As it has always been my method not to repeat myself, I have tried out new things and themes set in new milieus as I have not done before. But I have also this desire to go back to the world of earlier times, like for instance in my next film, *The Home and the World—Ghare Bairey* by Rabindranath, which is a political story with a political background, the first terrorist movement in 1905 over the partition of Bengal. I think it is interesting to be able to recreate an earlier period. That's an interest in itself; carrying out research on the period, on the furniture, on the dress, on the speech—this in itself is a preoccupation of mine.

BENEGAL: Then it must be more than nostalgia.

RAY: It's not nostalgia. I don't think it's nostalgia, it's taking up a sort of a challenge, like in *Shatranj ke Khiladi*. Well, it was interesting to grapple with this problem of showing something which happened in the middle of the nineteenth century, and to view it from perhaps a contemporary point of view, from an attitude. It is not just a straight recreation from what's in the book. It is a recreation filtered through my own personality which is, I think, a middle-of-the-twentieth-century personality.

BENEGAL: There is a criticism from some quarters that you have been a little too even-handed in *Shatranj* between the colonial masters and the Indians in the story. How do you react to that?

RAY: I don't agree with that. It's just that I felt it would be so easy to run down the colonial representative—it would have been an easy target, and I'm not interested in easy targets really. The point is made nevertheless, but it was necessary, it was interesting, I think, to show a colonial representative having his personal qualms about what he was supposed to be doing.

BENEGAL: The criticism, I think, is based on the assumption that for the colonized people, the only valid attitude is one where you would want to get rid of the colonial masters, and the critics make the point that in this kind of a situation the attitude appeared to be a bit even-handed.

RAY: Yes, but the ultimate point that the film was trying to make was that the two representatives of the Nawabi class were willing to carry on with their game of chess and not so anxious to get the colonialists out of their way. It was their non-involvement that was made responsible up to a certain extent for what happened. The annexation and the whole business of how the British were able to do what they did were because of certain traits in the Indian character itself.

Dialects in Dialogues

BENEGAL: You have so many dialects in Bengali. How do you use them in your films?

RAY: Well, in my urban stories I try to retain the dialect as far as possible, in the sense that, for instance, the North Calcuttans would speak a different kind of Bengali from the South Calcutta people, or people who have migrated from East Bengal would retain in their speech a lot of the East Bengal accent. All that one has to keep in mind. But when dealing with the village one uses the convention of a roughly rural speech without being too regional, consciously regional. Even in older or other Bengali films, in the films from Saratchandra Chattopadhyay and other Bengali writers who had written about village life, they would use a kind of speech which would not be too strongly a dialect, but be a sort of general rural dialogue which was accepted as a convention. We didn't depart from that, we used that in *Ashani*

Sanket, which, for instance, is supposed to have been laid in the region of Birbhum where the speech is not like what is used in the film really. But then I don't identify the place too much because most of the villages look alike anyway.

Women

BENEGAL: Mr Ray, most of your films have dealt with change actually. Your characters, your main characters are usually either coping with or adapting to this change. It starts with your trilogy and carries all the way through to *Jana Aranya*. When you have dealt with that, you have also dealt with women in *Charulata* and *Mahanagar*, and how they are coping with change. But beyond that I don't think you have done very much work about women in films. Why are you not interested?

RAY: Well, I'm trying to think what I've done actually. In the trilogy of course Apu was the main character, then *Jalsaghar, Parashpathar, Abhijaan*—all films about men really in the centre. *Mahanagar* presumably was the first film (about a woman), although in *Devi* you had this young girl who, you know, was a victim of circumstances, not so much change; well, change also in a way, but not in the sense *Mahanagar* is about change or *Charulata* is about change. After *Mahanagar* and *Charulata, Kapurush* to a certain extent is about the same thing. Then what did we have? Then we had the Calcutta stories which deal mainly with jobless young men or men with jobs. No, it's not that I'm not very interested in that question, but it's just that I didn't come across an interesting enough story. My next film, *The Home and the World*, is again about a woman in the centre, and about change, very much about change. But it's just one of those things, because I've been doing all kinds of different things over the years.

From Story to Script to Film

BENEGAL: I have another question which is of a technical nature, a question from a director. In *Sadgati* you have a rain sequence. Now since you always carefully work out your scripts and your scenes and so on well in advance—and particularly on location where not everything is likely to go right, what happens when nature provides opportunities like this? What do you do?

RAY: Well, if it provides an opportunity which fits the story or may even improve the original, it would be accepted as an improvement on the original conception. For instance, in the scene which I think you refer to, where the chamar's wife comes to her husband's dead body, the rain was supposed to come much later. The rain was supposed to start at night, when the brahmans, husband and wife, can't make up their minds about what to do with the body. But since we had this downpour, this extraordinary downpour at the time of shooting during the day, we immediately decided: why not have the rain start earlier? We had to think immediately of what comes before and what comes after. There was a mental calculation which had to be done on the spot, and immediately we decided to use the rain. But of course there was the problem whether the rain would last that long. It did last that long, and there were three changes of setup and other considerable preparations, for instance, laying long tracks and all that. We were just lucky that the rain lasted for something like three quarters of an hour in which time we were able to take all those shots covering the entire scene. If we had not been able to do it, then we would probably have to reshoot it without rain. It has just so happened several times in the past. We have had such weather or certain sudden changes in climate that at the moment I felt that this would enhance the scene or be usable for a certain scene, and I would use it. That needed very quick preparations and very quick working out how it fits into the scheme of things, what comes before and what comes after, whether it upsets the continuity or not.

BENEGAL: Now with *Sadgati*, you have a story, where you have taken a very strong stand. I mean the film comes through with a tremendous amount of power and strength, and you do see oppression of a particular kind in full force. It isn't the kind of your gentle, the more ironic look at things. Is this a kind of new trend you see in your own work?

RAY: If I had found a story like *Sadgati* earlier I would have certainly done it. It's just that the story called for that kind of treatment because that force, that anger is already there in the original story. And it seemed absolutely right for this particular story. It didn't need the softening of contours. I mean it had to be hard-edged. I really don't know, I haven't worked it out whether this is a sort of inner change in myself, a looking at things in a more harsh sort of way than in an oblique way. It's just that this style seemed absolutely right for *Sadgati*, and it's exactly how Premchand conceived the story. I've made almost no changes [to the story] except perhaps add a few scenes here and there.